"A most helpful, intimate story of one man's journey facing life, death, and the letting go of attachments."
—Gerald G. Jampolsky, M.D.,
author of *Out of Darkness Into the Light*

"A book of healing all the more powerful for the writer being a man. . . . When a loved one dies we are forced to take birth once again. This is such a story. There is no quick Phoenix here—just the deep, painful work of coming back to life."
—Stephen Levine,
author of *Meetings at the Edge* and *Who Dies*

"There has been a great gap in the grieving literature on the male experience of grief. Lon has shared his pain and hope from the deepest levels of his self. . . . I will certainly recommend WHY HER WHY NOW to my clients, both male and female."
—Nancy O'Connor, Ph.D.,
author of *Letting Go With Love*

"Riding the roller coaster of grief with Lon Elmer, one can appreciate that the only thing to hold on to, from moment to moment, is the light of one's own truth."
—Ram Dass,
author of *Journey of Awakening*

WHY HER WHY NOW

WHY HER WHY NOW

A MAN'S JOURNEY
THROUGH LOVE AND DEATH
AND GRIEF

LON ELMER

BANTAM BOOKS
NEW YORK · TORONTO · LONDON · SYDNEY · AUCKLAND

WHY HER WHY NOW
A Bantam Book / published by arrangement with the author

PRINTING HISTORY
Signal Elm Press edition published 1987

Acknowledgment is made to the following for their kind permission to reprint copyrighted material: From OUT ON A LIMB by Shirley MacLaine. © 1983 by Shirley MacLaine. Reprinted by permission of Bantam Books, Inc. From ON DEATH AND DYING by Elisabeth Kubler-Ross. © 1970 by Elisabeth Kubler-Ross. Reprinted by permission of Macmillan Publishing Co. From THE BOOK OF MIRDAD, THE STRANGE STORY OF A MONASTERY WHICH WAS ONCE CALLED THE ARK by Mikhail Naimy. © 1962 by Mikhail Naimy. Reprinted by permission of Clear Press, London in association with Element Books, Salisbury. 1984 Edition. From THE WAY OF LIFE ACCORDING TO LAO TZU translated by Witter Bynner. © 1944 by Witter Bynner. Reprinted by permission of Putman Publishing Group. From WHO DIES? by Stephen Levine. © 1982 by Stephen Levine. Excerpts reprinted by permission of Doubleday & Co. From CREATIVE DIVORCE: A NEW OPPORTUNITY FOR PERSONAL GROWTH by Mel Krantzler. © 1973, 1974 by Mel Krantzler. Reprinted by permission of the publisher, M. Evans & Co. 216 E. 49th St., New York, NY. From "DON'T FALL OFF THE MOUNTAIN" by Shirley MacLaine. © 1970 by Shirley MacLaine. Reprinted by permission of W. W. Norton & Co., Inc. From MEETINGS AT THE EDGE by Stephen Levine. © 1984 by Stephen Levine. Reprinted by permission of Doubleday & Co. From THE GLOBAL BRAIN by Peter Russell. © 1983 by Peter Russell. Reprinted by permission of J. P. Tarcher, Inc. From THE KABIR BOOK: FORTY-FOUR OF THE ECSTATIC POEMS OF KABIR, version by Robert Bly. © 1971, 1977 by Robert Bly. Reprinted by permission of the Seventies Press. From A COMPENDIUM OF SWEDENBORG'S THEOLOGICAL WRITINGS by Samuel Warren. © 1979 by Swedenborg Foundation, Inc. Reprinted by permission of the Swedenborg Foundation, Inc. From HEAVEN AND HELL by Emanuel Swedenborg, translated by George Dole. © 1971, 1979 by the Swedenborg Foundation, Inc. Reprinted by permission of the Swedenborg Foundation, Inc.

Bantam New Age and the accompanying figure design as well as the statement "the search for meaning, growth and change" are trademarks of Bantam Books, a division of Bantam Doubleday Dell Publishing Group, Inc.

Bantam edition / February 1990

Library of Congress Cataloging-in-Publication Data

Elmer, Lon.
  Why her, why now : a man's journey through love, and death, and grief / Lon Elmer.
    p.   cm.
  ISBN 0-553-34834-5
  1. Bereavement—Religious aspects.   2. Grief.   3. Widowers—Psychology.   4. Elmer, Lon.   5. Elmer, Nancy Pema Madson, 1940–1983   I. Title.
BL65.B47E43   1990
155.9′37—dc20   89-7014
                                                                         CIP

Book design by M 'N O Production Services, Inc.

Published simultaneously in the United States and Canada

PRINTED IN THE UNITED STATES OF AMERICA

CWO   0 9 8 7 6 5 4 3 2 1

Dedicated To

Nancy Pema Madson Elmer

1940–1983

CONTENTS

SPECIAL ACKNOWLEDGMENTS

Thank you, dear friends, for being there when we needed you, especially Katherine, Stephen, Suzie, Peter, Mary, Barney and Loren.

Thank you, dear family, for your loving support.

Thank you, Keith, Ray, Uncle Cliff and you other men who shared your feelings regarding the death of a loved one.

Thank you, Sharon, Kathy, Barbara, Donna, Verla and Charles for your invaluable help in preparing this manuscript.

Thank you, Eulah and Jim for your vision.

Thank you, Carol, Jinny, David and George for your comments and support.

And thank you, Bill from the Danica support group, for saying, "I wish what you had just said was in a book."

PREFACE

On November 20, 1983, my wife, Nancy Pema Madson Elmer, died as a result of tissue degeneration in her lungs, hip, breast and liver—cancer. She is not the first person I have known who has died from cancer.

When I was about fifteen, I visited a favorite aunt in a Connecticut hospital. The last time I saw her, she was shriveled, just skin and bones, with her skin unusually darkened and her hair very thin and fragile looking. Her voice was weak and her eyes shone with a light that I did not understand. Soon after, she died.

Since then, I've witnessed with increasing frequency the demise of friends and acquaintances as they died from cancer. Seeing what they went through, I was able to observe patterns which, when they appeared with Nancy, allowed me to be a step ahead at critical times.

Of course it wasn't easy to be wrapped up in the multitude of subjective feelings which accompanied losing my beloved, while at the same time seeing objectively which specific symptoms were appearing and then drawing conclusions as to what would more than likely happen next. As it was, I had more feelings and emotions come up for me than I knew what to do with. So, I wrote them down, partly as a way to release them and partly as a way to keep track of what was happening to me/ to us. My journal became like a road map of where I'd been, a record of movement through this overwhelming experience.

Often I would experience something which others, most notably Elisabeth Kubler-Ross, Stephen Levine and those involved in death-and-dying investigations, have recorded in their books. Equally as often, something would happen, especially during Nancy's transition and after, which corresponded with teachings relating to death and the afterlife found in the major religions of the world. In a very real way, my/our experiences were corroborating their observations, and their observations were helping me/us through the experience. As events unfolded, I knew that I had to write them down.

Preparing this book has been like giving my heart a shower-bath, while my mind examines everything that is going down the drain. It has been great therapy, a refreshing release. It has also given me insights into the ways in which our culture inadvertently limits a man's grief process.

Men suffer. Men suffer deep sorrow and grief from losing a son, a daughter, a spouse to the slow death called cancer. Men suffer shock and unimaginable anguish as their families are slaughtered by other people on the highways of our nation. Men suffer pain and hopelessness as their friends and lovers die from AIDS. Men suffer rejection, confusion and emptiness as their dreams and hopes from a marriage are scattered in divorce. Men suffer anger and frustration over the loss of their livelihoods, as do the farmers and middle-managers being tossed aside by compassionless business. Men suffer depression and low self-esteem, as do our brothers still fighting the ghosts of Vietnam.

Often, too often, we men do our suffering in silence, behind closed doors, so that our women, our children and especially other men will not see us as appearing weak. We walk around in bodies stiff with armor, hard with tense neck, shoulder and back muscles, and a better than average likelihood of having some sort of heart disease. We have somehow gotten ourselves to believe that a man ain't supposed to cry, that a man can bear unlimited suffering, that a man is above pain and sorrow. We men have burdened ourselves with maintaining the Rambo or John Wayne caricature from our nation's mythological view of itself—the hard, strong man defending his woman and his value system from the heathens without a whimper, shiver, or tear. However, inside of this cultural image is a human being with feelings, hurt, pain and grief.

Feelings are neuter; they are not sexually defined. Only our narrow notions of what a man is (and of what a woman is) define whether or not our feelings are expressed.

Through this book, I am sharing how I went through my grief. Perhaps this will give you insights into how you can feel freer to express your own grief. Through this book, I am reaching out to others who share my conclusion that the significance of death lies in its ability to give meaning to life and that there is an inherent joy to be found in recognizing the transition of a loved one's soul.

This book is for you who have had similar thoughts and feelings, but have had to push them down deep inside yourself in order to act out the expectations of others. Perhaps you are finding those imposed limitations have left you feeling frustrated and alone and maybe even cheated out of more fully experiencing one of life's most profound events—the death of a loved one.

In closing, I need to say that I am truly grateful for the agony and joy that Nancy and I shared and for the tumble of intense feelings that I am still going through.

Thank You, Lord, for this most profound, painful, joyful, exasperating, exhausting, exciting, draining, enlightening, disrupting and wondrous learning experience.

Lon Elmer
Seattle, Washington
December 1986

. . . and he who remains passive when overwhelmed with grief loses his best chance of recovering elasticity of mind.

CHARLES DARWIN (1809–1882)
THE EXPRESSION OF THE EMOTIONS IN MAN AND ANIMALS

INTRODUCTION

The evening of Thanksgiving 1979, Nancy Pema Madson looked out over the skyline of Manhattan and pondered the words her spiritual teacher had given her. She did not realize that she was ending a decade's worth of spiritual study, intense meditation and inspired wanderings that had taken her from the Woodstock festival to the land of the Hopis. Her teacher had said to her, "Go home and take care of your mother." Nancy drove back to San Diego in time for Christmas. Among other gifts she received that year was $35.

On the first day of a new decade in Seattle, Lon Elmer woke up with the words of a former minister ringing in his ears. "What you do on the first day of a new year determines what you will do for that entire year," Pastor Neumeyer had said.

"This year, 1980, I will make money," Lon announced to the ceiling. He called his friend Michael in San Diego and asked him to set up a Polarity Therapy Workshop in three weeks for Lon to teach.

About mid-January, Nancy was checking out at the counter of the local health food store. The clerk reached under the counter and pulled out a piece of yellow paper. "This is for you," she said as she gave it to Nancy.

It read, "Polarity Therapy Workshop, given by Lon Elmer of Seattle. Learn to balance your vital energy with exercises, diet and manipulations. Contact Michael at 323-3223 for details. Cost $35."

On the day of the workshop, Nancy was the first to arrive. At the end of the workshop she made an appointment for her mother to receive a private energy-balancing session with Lon. During the session, which Nancy had requested to observe, Nancy and Lon's eyes met. There were no barriers. There was complete openness, soul to soul connection. They fell in love. After a five minute conversation, she and her mother left, and he went back to Seattle.

They became engaged by telephone in April. In mid-May, Lon was on the East Coast beginning the preparations for their upcoming wedding in June. They had decided to marry in Pennsylvania in order to accommodate Lon's large family which lived in the area and Nancy's friends who lived around New York. Her mother, sister and brother-in-law agreed to the plan, as it would give them a chance to visit an area of the country with which they were unfamiliar.

On May 24th, two days before her anticipated arrival on the East Coast, Nancy told Lon that she had just learned that she had a malignant tumor, that she had cancer. They cried into their telephones 3,000 miles apart. Lon said, "I still love you. We are getting married. I'll see you at the airport in two days. And we'll decide what to do about the cancer after we're together."

They married on June 28, 1980, in a clearing in the woods behind his aunt's house, surrounded by friends and relations. He was 39, she was 40. They felt like Two Virgins, just like John and Yoko.

During the less than four years that Nancy and Lon were together they had a beautiful, love-filled life that was increasingly overshadowed by the demands of Nancy's cancer. She had the unanticipated (and unwanted) opportunity to put all of her spiritual understanding regarding death and the transition of one's soul into practice. He had the opportunity to learn to accept that his expectations were meaningless, that what really mattered were the needs of the moment. As their backgrounds, trainings and understandings blended together to support Nancy as she died and Lon as he grieved, their experience gave new strength to the notion that there are no accidents.

As Lon put it, "I began to believe more and more that I was being utilized by the Lord to facilitate Nancy's soul's transition." Here is his story.

THREE YEARS
AFTER—NOVEMBER 1986

Earlier today, I pulled a well-traveled suitcase out of the closet. An Army surplus belt tied around its bruised, dirty, white body insures that it will not spill its contents when I lift it. The clasps hold on valiantly, their brass plating long gone; they welcome the belt's help. Loops of wire wrapped with foam rubber and masking tape hang in the fasteners where the handle formerly stood. Embossed in the leather between the handle fasteners, you can still see three letters, N.L.M., even though the gold leaf is but a whisper of its former self.

This suitcase is all that remains from the set of luggage that Nancy Lu Madson—the valedictorian speaker, class of 1957, Helix High School—received as a graduation gift one sunny June day. She took her clothes and her dreams in those suitcases to the University of Redlands that fall. She began a journey that took her to Yosemite as a summer waitress, to the University of Washington for an M.A. in Sociology, to a Yale coffee house where she strummed her guitar and sang folk songs, to Albertus Magnus College where she taught the *I Ching*, to the Meditation Center in Barre, Massachusetts, to the Zen community in Sharon Springs, New York, to the Tibetan Buddhist Monastery in Woodstock, New York, where she immersed herself in spiritual studies, and to Seattle where we shared married life.

I always get weepy when I open her suitcase. In it are reminders of the woman I fell in love with, the vibrant, alive, intelligent, creative, beautiful woman I married. I don't open it too often. It hurts too much. Seeing and holding her things stirs up my sadness and resurrects feelings of loss. I empty the suitcase carefully, reverently, for these things are the tangible remnants of a life and a relationship.

The mother-of-pearl decorated wooden box from India contains our love letters. The white box next to it holds invitations and napkins from our wedding. I remember the day we selected the stationery for our invitations; a friend did the calligraphy, I drew the map. It was the same day I bought her a nightgown, and she tried on a bikini—at my insistence. She was shy and quite embarrassed. We didn't buy it. Weeks later, she confessed to going back to the store to buy the bikini in order to surprise me. But it was gone, she told me with a mixture of disappointment and relief.

Here are a stack of photographs: Nancy as a flag-twirler in high school, her high school graduation picture (her Southern California blond hair and tan surrounding her heart-melting smile), Nancy with Ram Dass, Nancy being Pema, the yoga practitioner, in the Bahamas (she adopted Pema, which means lotus, as her spiritual name) and Christmas with her sister one month before we met. In an antique embroidered bag, I find small seashells which she had beach-combed and miniature pottery—favorite pieces from her collection of items for her puja table, her meditation shrine.

A program from the University of Redlands Christmas Cantata, in which Nancy sang in the chorus, covers a stack of drawings and watercolors of Hindu gods and goddesses which she drew. Under them are notebooks filled with page after hand-lettered page of Buddhist prayers and mantras, souvenirs, so to speak, of a disciplined, diligent, decade-long search for truth and understanding.

At the bottom of the suitcase are her unique creations: photo books in which her photographs are placed in kaleidoscopic patterns so that the subject of the photograph breaks out of the ordinary and dazzles the viewer with incredible beauty. Nancy had the imagination and the ability to convert a photo of the front end of her car into a vibrant, shining star.

Practically everything in this suitcase is alive with color. Yet you'd never know it by looking at just the outside. These colorful, unique bits and pieces are what attracted me to her. I liked what I saw then and I wanted to see more.

Our relationship was born in instant love—Cupid shot his arrows, and they hit their mark—and fueled by our mutual "likes." We went into an immediate marriage (for which I have no regrets) and discovered our likes and dislikes within the framework of a committed relationship. We shared in the joys of mutual discovery as she created new works of art and I created good "deals" by which we furnished our home.

After awhile, however, I began to lose contact with the details of the Nancy I had initially fallen in love with as they disappeared under the weight of her increasing cancer. Nancy became less and less someone I had hoped to know better and more and more someone I really had not wanted in my life so soon. My hopes for a stable, fruitful, lifetime relationship were dashed on the rocks of reality. Instead, I got to know Nancy as she suffered the fears, anger, frustration and disappointment of a woman with a catastrophic disease.

Her slow shift from an independent, self-supporting, creative, vivacious woman of the world to a dependent, bed-ridden victim of pain-inflicting cancer was not without its bumps and knocks. For example, she insisted on keeping her job because, she argued, we needed the money. I insisted she stop work and stay home and take care of herself. We would argue about it. Eventually the truth became clear. Her working was not about money. She needed her job in order to maintain her integrity by being a person functioning in society. To give up her job under these circumstances would be to give up her self-image of being someone who contributes to society. She had been self-supporting most of her adult life. Any threat to her abilities to maintain herself met with stiff resistance.

She showed her determination over and over again as she went through her daily routine, her self-designed "wellness program" which she hoped would carry her to victory in her battle against cancer. Every day she would do a sequence of self-administered techniques which she (and I) had found in the extensive literature on alternate ways to deal with cancer. She chose to be actively responsible for her own health instead of passively accepting the decisions of a medical doctor.

In spite of Nancy's valiant and determined efforts and the efforts and advice of those professionals she chose to assist her with her "wellness program," she died.

As I repack her suitcase, tears well up in my eyes. A brown envelope is the last item in, just as it was three years ago. It contains her death certificate.

1983

KING LEAR

I have a life-long interest in Shakespeare's play *King Lear*. Ever since first reading it in high school, I have never ceased to be fascinated with this man Lear as he loses his ego and discovers his self.

Briefly, we meet Lear as king of all he surveys. In his dotage, he gives his kingdom to his two eldest daughters. Since most men don't like to volunteer to lose, Lear proceeds with the assumption that even though he will no longer be involved in the daily workings of the kingdom, he will still be treated royally. The daughters—who had won Lear over by stroking his ego— take him at his kingly word and take over the kingdom lock, stock and barrel, leaving Lear stripped of all he had found identification in.

Ultimately, Lear ends up huddled in a windbreak at the top of a cliff during a furious storm. His only company is a fool, a madman and a blind man. In this situation—stripped of all he thought he was—Lear ceases living on the surface of life and dives deep inside to discover who and what he really is. He has his enlightenment when he realizes that his third daughter— his youngest, whom he disinherited because she would not stroke his vanity—was offering unconditional love to the man inside the kingly trappings. He then begins living in the kingdom of the heart, his inner essence, instead of in the kingdom of the world.

During my career as a drug abuse counselor, I often thought of King Lear as I worked with people who were undergoing the death of their image of themselves while on drugs—the so-called LSD death trip. They saw themselves dying. They became disoriented, lost in the limitless potential for their lives that their egos had prevented them from seeing. My job was to guide them away from the edge of the cliff, to prevent them from succumbing to their fears.

Now, as my wife rests fitfully beside me, I again think of King Lear. Like him, I am being stripped of all I hold near and dear, of all I hold important. Like him, I feel caught up in a wild storm which is pushing me to the edge of a precipice over which lies I don't know what. And, like Lear, I may very well end up discovering who and what I really am.

Maybe the tragedy of the human race was that we had forgotten we were each Divine. And if we realized that, we could dispel fear from our lives. In dispelling fear, we could dispel hate. And much more. With the fear, we would rid ourselves of greed and war and killing. Fear was the root and circle around which our lives revolved—fear of failure, fear of pain, fear of humiliation, fear of loneliness, fear of being unloved, fear of ourselves, fear of death, ultimately fear of fear. Fear itself was insidious, infectious, seeping in from one point of unreality to permeate all our lives. Perhaps our belief in death was the greatest unreality of all. If we could truly know that we never really died, that we always got another chance, that no pain, no humiliation, no loss was ever final, total and forever, maybe we could understand that there was nothing to fear.

SHIRLEY MACLAINE
OUT ON A LIMB

SOUL TALK

One day in 1983, my teacher gave me a lesson which helped me to understand what was happening to Nancy and what was happening to me. His explanation of how things are felt good to me, as if my soul were resonating with it. This is what he said:

"A person is a unique entity. Each person is a manifested soul. Each soul is complete and mature, capable of manifesting God's Will through its physical body in this world. The free will we humans have is the soul deciding whether or not to manifest (be a channel for) God's Will.

"The bite from the apple in the Garden of Eden marked the separation of the soul from God by means of manifestation to the physical. It takes a mouth on a body to bite, especially something as hard as an apple. Right?" I agreed. He went on, "From that point on, soul became enmeshed in the physical, as exemplified by awareness of an embarrassment over those most physical of body parts, the genitals. The genitals are those parts of the physical body whose sole function is to reproduce the physical form. In order to guarantee the continued reproduction of the species, the reproductive act is pleasurable.

"The soul progresses from the Brightest of Light, where it is at one with God, to the physical plane, where it is given its opportunity to learn something. This could be called the 'fall from grace.' In the physical plane, the soul, through its physical manifestation, learns what it needs in order to be with God again. The lesson could be being generous, honest, compassionate, forgiving, loving, etc., or simply accepting that there is more going on in our universe than simply meets the eye or than can be proven in the mind-oriented so-called 'scientific' sense.

"When a soul manifests in the human form, it, the soul, is complete and in control of this 'new' vehicle, this biological environmental adaptation," he said, thumping his body. "The soul," he continued, "tells us when its physical form is hungry or needs its diapers changed or when it wants to be held like it used to be 'held' when it was at one with God. We, being adults and therefore smarter, teach the physical form to use toys, to use tools, to use language. In this training, we awaken the child's brain by giving it information to process: how to use toys, how to use tools, how to use language, who and how to love, who and how to hate. At some point, the *mind* wakes up. The mind is that part of the brain which is aware of thoughts and how to use them. From this, the *ego* is born, the ego being that part of the mind which says, 'Only I can be, do, see, hear, smell, feel, think this way.' In other words, the ego is created when the mind takes itself seriously.

"During this process of transferring awareness from the soul to the ego, the soul's influence lessens noticeably. The soul's reason for being here in the first place gets lost in the shuffle. In the meantime, the mind, whose sole function is to be the shop foreman keeping the physical body operating efficiently and effectively, has convinced itself that it owns the factory and can therefore dictate policy. That's what the ancients call the world of illusion. It's this allowing our lives to be directed by a functionary in the chain-of-command, instead of by our soul (who has come here to learn and practice love, generosity, compassion, caring, honesty, trust, etc.), that accounts for the human experience being mired in the mud of negativity, both individually and collectively. And an aspect of this mud is disease, dis-ease, lack of ease.

"Newborn babies' eyes are so clear. They are souls who are practicing unconditional trust and unconditional love. When we look into their eyes, we can see, if we care to see that far, all the way back to God. The eyes are the windows of the soul. That's an old saying and a true one. The eyes are also the only part of the nervous system on the surface, exposed. The eyes can and do show us the condition of the physical form and of the mind when examined with the understanding of iridology and other similar studies. You know that young beings are attracted to light. It reminds them of from whence they came. Too often the source of the light is a light bulb or reflections off of eyeglasses or television. Well, little soul, welcome to the physical plane. Be wary to not confuse content for intent.

"As a being grows, the physical becomes dominant. Wellness occurs, as does illness. Sometimes illness occurs after several years of physical manifestation, sometimes after a few. Some, such as the so-called 'children's diseases,' are caused by improper nourishment. Others, such as cancer, are soul lessons; they're the soul having to go through this way of detaching from the physical. I remember you telling me about Nancy's recurring dream, the one in which she sees herself as an old woman covered with sores. That old woman is Nancy's soul in an earlier incarnation; she too died from cancer. In the old woman's case, she rejected the disease, denied that she had it. She became obsessed with it and spent all of her time denying that she was dying. She spent no time preparing for her transition. So, she had to go through it again.

"Paul Tuttle, who lives near here, channels an entity named Raj. According to Raj, each soul is responsible for the condition of the physical form it inhabits. At the spiritual level, a soul can direct the course a body will take. Thus, if there is a physical problem, the soul working through the mind can direct and authorize that the problem be corrected. And it will. However, should the mind doubt (thinks it owns the factory and can therefore dictate policy), the physical problem cannot and will not be corrected. Interesting, yes? Thus, the mind can be your best friend, or your worst enemy, depending on how much soul is allowed through.

"Consequently, when we see a fellow human being whose physical form is sick, we do all we can do to relieve the burden of their suffering. We are compassionate for what is happening. Yet, it is not for us to feel responsible for the person's recovery or demise. What ultimately happens is determined by how the soul interprets the Will of God.

"By the way," he said, looking at me, "How is Nancy?"

I looked into his compassionate face and said, "She's dying."

"And how do you feel about it?" he asked.

"I'm not really certain," I answered hesitantly. "I think I feel threatened."

"That's your mind talking," he said. "Listen to your heart. How do you feel?"

"Scared," I said.

"I understand," he said and poured me a cup of tea.

TERMINAL

Ram Dass tells the story of a town under attack in which all monks are being disemboweled by the attackers. On hearing of the approaching attackers, the remaining monks ran from the monastery and hid in the hills. Except for one monk. As the general of the marauding troops threw open the gate of the monastery and swaggered inside, he was greeted by the solitary monk standing in the middle of the courtyard. The general, with his sword in his hand, went to the monk and with his meanest facial expression, looked the monk in the eye and said, "Do you know that I can take my sword and slice your belly wide open without even blinking an eye?"

The monk paused a moment, then responded, "Do you know that I can let you take your sword and slice my belly wide open without blinking an eye?"

Clearly, we are not all monks. If we were, we would probably be hiding in the hills with the rest of them. Thinking about being disemboweled gives me the shivers—in my gut, interestingly enough. (Perhaps that's why our culture finds *hari-kari* so hard to stomach.) This story deals with the Biggie, DEATH, and how to cope with it. The hiding monks fear death. The solitary monk accepts death. Ultimately, we are all going to die. We are all terminal. It's just that some of us are more obvious about it than others. How we accept our death when it happens is up to us. Now, while we are still alive, is our opportunity to prepare for that moment of truth.

Probably the most difficult part of dealing with the loss of a loved one is having to accept your own death. When I was younger, I tended to view myself as living forever. I had no concept of death. Then one day, I found my pet goldfish floating dead in his bowl. Later, a grandmother I hardly knew died. To me in my young world, old people and little animals died, but not me.

During my eighth grade year, an acquaintance didn't come to school one day. He'd hung himself. I didn't think much about it. Later on, my high school science project partner died in an automobile accident. It meant nothing to me. I felt no remorse. I was alive and planning on living forever. The exuberance of youth. The exuberance of being infinite.

Finally one day soon after my cousin died (his was the first death in my generation of the family), I realized that I too was going to die; that I too am finite; that my body, the superb environmental adaptation and temple of God that it is, will cease to function. Believe me, it was not easy to say, "I will die, I will cease to live." It was difficult to accept that my death is only a breath away, that life is really a gift from God that can end at any moment, that I too am terminal.

My mind went into fear. "I don't want to die. I have so much to live for. I have so much I still need to do. There are so many things I want to accomplish. My family will be distraught. I don't want to make them unhappy (by dying). I like being alive and here on this planet. Death will take away my control of my life. (Maybe that's why people commit suicide, to gain control over their lives by having control over when they die.) And what will happen to me when I die?" Then came repugnant images of my body decaying or being cremated or eaten by worms. And of course, the classic claustrophobic fear of waking up in a coffin six feet under. My mind had a field day digging up all those fears until I remembered an old saying about the mind: your mind can be either your best friend or your worst enemy. With that, I saw that my mind's running around in fear was being an enemy to my overall well being and that I needed to switch to something more positive.

I went out for a walk. I like to walk. I found a penny. I'm always finding money laying around. On the penny it says, "In

God We Trust." BAM! The positive thought I needed. In God We Trust. Trust in the Lord, and the Lord will provide. Trust, Trust, Trust. Give up needing to be in control. Let go, let God. Relax. Put your life in God's hands. All that stuff I've heard for years. Letting go of my need to be in control of every cell and second of my life. The big thing to do is trust. Trust that there is a greater power (the Force, Cosmic Consciousness, God, Universal Energy, the Tao, Yahweh, etc.) and trust that there is a Divine Use which we are all doing whether we recognize it or not. We all have our place in the scheme of things, our place being that unique expression of the human experience that each one of us is.

That penny made it clear to me that it is much easier to give up the need for control of every little aspect of my life and to trust in a higher power now, while I'm still alive, rather than jamming it all into that final second when death takes control whether I like it or not.

So, for me, fear was replaced by trust. That satisfied my heart's acceptance of my body's finite nature. To satisfy my mind, I read spiritual and theological literature which continually affirms that our greatest human lesson is to learn to trust and, after having learned to trust, to accept whatever happens as exactly what needs to happen. In other words, trust in the Lord, and the Lord will provide; and then accept that what is provided is what you really need in order to grow to a higher level of consciousness, i.e., a higher level of understanding and appreciation for what already is right now, this very moment. Ahh, what a weight off my shoulders. The struggle is no more.

About a year after Nancy died, I had an experience that confirmed my thoughts on fear. I walked on fire. I walked barefoot on hot, burning coals. A fire walking workshop was held nearby, and I attended it. As it turned out, the actual fire walk was more like an exclamation point on the end of a sentence. The important stuff, the body of the sentence, took place during the hours preceding the walk. For four hours we dealt with fear. We shared fears, like what was the worst possible thing that could happen to us. The lady next to me was afraid of falling into the fire and being disfigured, having her face horribly burnt. I shared that one too, as did others. As we went around the group and got into our levels of fear, I saw that my biggest fear at that moment was writing a letter I had successfully put off for six months.

After sharing our fears and doing other preparatory things, we went out to the fire. It had become a bed of red-hot, glowing coals—perfect for marshmallows and hot dogs. One by one, we walked through the coals. I watched as others did it first. I had to see it done before I'd do it. Then, as my inner voice said "Go," I went to the edge of the fire pit, felt the warmth from the coals and, trusting my inner voice, I converted fear from a barrier to an ally and walked across the hot, glowing coals.

I'm not sure how I did it, but it's something like this. Fear as a barrier says, "Do not walk into traffic because you can get killed." Thus, fear prevents us from crossing the street, which limits the size of our world considerably. Fear as an ally, like a parrot on your shoulder, says, "Look both ways before crossing the street, then cross as traffic permits." Converting fear from a barrier/obstacle to an ally/helper requires stepping out of the net of unfavorable possibilities that the mind is busy casting about and stepping into the inner awareness that is sensitive to the still, small voice inside. You do not confront your fear. There is no attempt to battle with it or to overcome it. To attempt to subdue one's fear through confrontation makes you a walking civil war because it takes energy, your energy, to feed both the fear and that which you have marshaled against your fear. It's much easier to make fear your friend, to learn from it and to use it to help you attain your goals. This comes from the Chinese concept of effortless effort, *wu-wei.*

When I listened to my still, small voice inside, and it said "Go," I went. I walked across the fire pit and I did it again so that my mind could see that I had actually done it—without blinking an eye.

Walking on fire was what I needed to do to confirm that I had learned to trust. I had learned to trust my inner voice and I had learned to trust God. Trust alone did not carry me across the hot, burning coals; my feet did. However, trust was the key that unlocked what I needed to do to get to the other side. Trusting in the Lord by itself does not carry me through my grief, but it does open the way for the creative power, courage and love to come through to meet every situation.

I accept that I will die. I accept that my body will cease to be. I accept that, as much as I like it here, there will come a time when I will no longer be a living, breathing environmental adaptation working, playing, loving, fearing, hating, collecting, walking, talking, writing, seeing movies, driving my car, watching the sun rise and set on this lovely planet Earth. I trust that my fear regarding death will be a friend and ally to guide me through death instead of being an obstacle that prevents me from focusing all of my attention and energy on what is taking place, my soul's transition to the spiritual realms.

By accepting the reality of my own death, that I am terminal, and by converting my fear of death from a barrier that prevents me from living fully to a helper who shows me the way, I was able to be clear in my support of my dear wife, Nancy, as her death became imminent.

First Stage: Denial and Isolation
Second Stage: Anger
Third Stage: Bargaining
Fourth Stage: Depression
Fifth Stage: Acceptance

. . . the different stages people go through when they are faced with tragic news—defense mechanisms in psychiatric terms, coping mechanisms to deal with extremely difficult situations. These means will last for different periods of time, and will replace each other or exist at times side by side. The one thing that usually persists through all these stages is hope.

ELISABETH KUBLER-ROSS
ON DEATH AND DYING

WHAT YOUR LOVED ONE
IS GOING THROUGH

There is no way I can write down all the things that are happening with your loved one. We all have our own life histories to work through. Each one has his or her own assemblage of individual, specific details which make the unique human being he or she is. What I'll present here is an overview, a sequence of events which most people dying of cancer experience. This is based on readings and on talks with cancer patients and care givers.

Most, if not all, people dying from cancer go through a period which I compare to a roller coaster. It's not so much that there are ups and downs, which there are, it's more on the order of each up or peak being lower than the one preceding it. For example, Walter, a friend whose cancer death occurred six months before Nancy's, demonstrated this pattern most clearly. Later observation of Nancy and others supported this pattern.

One day Walter felt great. I met him in the lobby. He was dressed to the teeth and waiting for his friend to pick him up for lunch. Several days later, he was feeling so depressed that I didn't know he was around until I visited him in his apartment. A week later, we met in the lobby again while getting our mail. Although he admitted to not being very hungry, he was still neatly dressed. Another period of no contact followed. One day I saw him in the lobby, disheveled and in his pajamas. Once more, a period of no contact. A week later I met his friend in the lobby, who told me that Walter had called him after a period of silence and had invited him over. Soon after, Walter died.

With Nancy, her peaks and valleys were, for me, more closely observable. One peak, she made lunch for us. The next peak, we ate lunch together at the table, but I prepared it. The level of her peaks lessened so that eventually, her getting up and going to the bathroom became a peak experience. The energy-draining nature of cancer is such that what we as "well" people consider mundane experiences become peak experiences for the dying person.

After this series of ups and downs, which can last anywhere from weeks to months, there comes the final stage—the plateau. A plateau is a flat-topped hill. Thus, this peak lasts for awhile, rather than being a high point clearly defined by its being followed very quickly by a descent. The plateau is characterized by the dying person clearly feeling better, performing routine matters, and becoming actively involved in the lives of others. Because the loved one is behaving so differently from the preceding roller coaster, family and friends frequently think the hoped-for miracle has occurred, that the person is getting better. It's a false hope. Yet, the feeling of optimism that sweeps through is a refreshing change that momentarily lightens the load of the worriers. (The worriers are those who can't see the person for the disease.) The plateau ends abruptly, within a week or two, in a rapid descent which culminates in death.

That's the pattern we saw. Ups and downs in which each up is lower than the one before it, followed by a plateau, a leveling off at a level recognizably higher than the ups immediately preceding it, then a swift decline to death.

Meanwhile, as the support person(s) is (are) watching this pattern unfold, the person dying is going through their own inner sequence which starts with rejection/denial. There is a conscious denial of having cancer, a rejection of the illness. This rejection could be expressed as, "This is not actually happening. I don't have lung cancer, I have pneumonia," denying what it is. For the longest time, Nancy (and I, caught up in her enthusiasm) did not accept that the cancer was spreading. We felt it was under control, that the tumor growth was stabilized and that the other physical discomforts were secondary illnesses caused by the overall weakening of her body's immune system. Unfortunately, our medical advisors played into this false hope by not conveying to us what was really happening. Perhaps they deliberately held back information from her in order not to upset her. It was only in private consultations during which I persuaded the doctors I could handle the truth that some of them told me exactly what was happening. Curiously, their reports did little more than confirm my own feelings about the reality of Nancy's condition. I then wrestled daily with the dilemma of telling her versus letting her discover for herself. I chose not to tell her because of the already tense emotional climate in which we were living. (Anyone who has lived with a terminally ill loved one knows how emotionally and physically draining it is.) When she realized it herself, I confirmed her feelings.

After realizing the futility of rejecting and denying what is, most people go into a period of anger often followed by severe depression. They express this period of resentment with the words, "Why me?" It's only natural that a person who has consciously or unconsciously plotted out a full life ending around age 90 would be angry, resentful, hurt and depressed by the prospect of perhaps not seeing their next birthday when they'd be 43, 22, or 7.

After the anger and depression comes the bargaining, usually with God. "If you . . . , then I'll . . ." It's like what Martin Luther did when caught under a tree during a severe thunder storm, where he promised to enter a monastery if the Lord would spare his life. Bargaining, for a terminally ill person, is a good sign. It shows that they recognize that they are in a serious situation, that they are terminally ill. Bargaining is part of acceptance of the illness and acceptance of the reality of the situation.

So, the sequence we went through was rejection/denial, anger/resentment, depression, bargaining, acceptance. Now all of this does not take place in a vacuum. It is not an objective, step-by-step, rational process. It's a process that entails emotional upheaval and emotional elimination as the person comes to grips with their deepest fears, their own frustrated expectations, and their ties with family and friends. It can involve releasing emotional garbage that has been held in for years.

At this time, it is important for the support person(s), i.e., the immediate family/friend/helper who is in daily contact with the dying person, to remember that this emotional elimination is not directed at him or her personally, even though the words used may make it seem that way. The closest person becomes the convenient target for this emotional vomit. It takes a lot of effort on the part of the support person to not get caught up in these intense emotional eliminations.

Sometimes I forgot what was happening and did take Nancy's emotional eliminations personally. This led to totally irrational dialogue that drew our energies into a negative vortex like a whirlpool that sucked us down into it, so that when it was over, we were totally exhausted and hadn't anything to show for it. These arguments were devastating. Fortunately, they didn't happen very often.

They'd usually follow the same pattern. She'd say, "I need your support."

I'd say, "I'm giving you all I can."

She would start crying, "I have to go elsewhere to get what I need."

I took this as a rejection of what I was doing for her and got angry. I'd say, "I'm working three jobs to keep all of this going," while thinking of all the money spent on pills, doctors, medications, lab work, hospitals, support equipment, etc.

On and on, back and forth, both of us clearly pushing each other's buttons. It isn't always easy to remain cool, calm and centered while the one you love, your second self, is throwing negativity couched in the words that tear into your own vulnerabilities. Those times I got caught in Nancy's emotional eliminations were the times in which unhealthy, i.e., unresolvable, arguments took place. These intense emotional battles, compounded by the erosion of our stamina caused by dealing daily with a disease which takes all and gives nothing, left us totally exhausted.

To sustain my physical self during this period, I took additional B-complex, vitamin C and calcium supplements to feed my over-stressed nervous system. Nancy was getting supplements through her regular program. We found that apple cider vinegar in apple juice with up to 10 drops of Ortho-Phos Drops (Ortho-Phosphoric acid) in it made a drink which could pull us out of severe depression within half an hour. We had to remember to rinse out our mouths with baking soda in water immediately after in order to neutralize the acid in our mouths, otherwise it would affect the tooth enamel. It was also important to not swallow the baking soda solution, as that would neutralize the acidic drink we had just taken. The doctor who told me of this explained that when we are detoxifying, our bodies are in an alkaline condition. If we become too alkaline, we get into intense eliminations and depression. To acidify our systems quickly, thus curtailing the eliminations and depression, we could take the above mentioned combination.

DIVORCE

I was getting burned out by the burden of being caught in a work rut, seeing our savings and earnings fly out the window every month, with only medical bills and bottles of pills to show for it, and by coming home to rest and finding myself living in a hospital with a very needing patient. I was Nancy's prime supporter, full-time nurse, part-time therapist and full-time housekeeper. Doing dishes, cooking, doing laundry, house cleaning, emptying bed pans, counseling and consoling Nancy, endless errands and acts of love all became one big blur in my exhausted head. Even the long walks I took to get away from the home situation were no longer enough. After many months of this, I began to review my options: (1) Nancy gets well; (2) Nancy dies; (3) things remain static; (4) divorce.

My personal fear was that things would remain exactly the way they were, indefinitely. However, by remembering that "this too shall pass," I resolved my fear. I dropped that option. I wanted her to get well and be the vivacious woman I had fallen in love with so that we could go back to living normal lives again. Yet it was clear that that would never be, that those days were past. Then I grappled with the idea of her dying. Her death would definitely end the suffering we were living in. And I considered divorce.

At first, the idea of divorce didn't seem all that unreasonable. I've met people with cancer whose spouses divorced them because of the strain caused by dealing daily with the disease. Certainly our society accepts divorce as a way out of unbearable situations. Yet, as I considered it, I ran headlong into my own resistance to the idea. I did not want a divorce from Nancy. I loved her very much. I still do. What I wanted was a divorce from the cancer. I wanted the cancer out of my life. It was consuming the woman I loved. It was consuming all of our resources.

Perhaps the most painful day of our lives was the day we got into one of our energy-wasting arguments. In this argument, I brought up the three alternatives I saw. She, like I, preferred number one, that she get well. She rejected number two. She did not want to die. She said she felt stronger every day and felt she was winning her battle with cancer. I kept to myself my observations of her deteriorating physical condition, that she was exhibiting the same pattern I had observed with friends and relatives in the End Game phase of cancer.

The third option, divorce, ignited a cathartic emotional release—for her. She cried and threw things and pulled out all the stops. I opted for closing down and waiting for the storm to subside. Like a prairie dweller riding out a tornado in his storm cellar, I retreated deep inside my head until the fury passed. I admit responsibility for sometimes saying or doing something that triggered her elimination of negative emotions, all in the good faith of sharing my feelings. I felt at a loss. I did not know what to do.

I saw her point. The cancer was in her, and she was with me. And, as much as I wished to the contrary, the reality was that in order to keep her, I had to accept her the way she was, no matter what the imperfection, no matter what the cost. So, I did. We made up and collapsed in each other's arms, quite exhausted. It was a heart-rending day for both of us, one that got to our bottom-line fears: hers, that I would leave her and eliminate her support system, thus forcing her back on her own at a time when she needed all the help she could get, and mine, that there was no end in sight to this seemingly endless drain of physical, financial, mental and emotional resources.

I was trying desperately to get some sort of control of the situation. Thus, I ran through my options/our options. What I neglected to remember was the option I had discovered on that found penny, to let go of control and let God run the show. Trusting God would force me to trust the process as it unfolded, since I would no longer be the one calling the shots. But since I wasn't calling the shots to begin with, trusting became the only realistic alternative.

As I gave myself over to trusting God, I began to learn what the process is and how it works, to discover what part I played in the whole thing and to then play my part to the best of my abilities. By trusting, I began to understand that it was no accident Nancy and I were together; the Lord had put us together for a specific purpose. And that purpose was for me to support the return of her soul back to God.

Looking back, I recall praying a lot, asking for the strength and courage to accept what had been given, and thanking the Lord for this opportunity to serve. I still do. Also, I feel an inner sense of peace from having stayed with Nancy and having given her my full, loving support all the way through to the end. I feel good for having given all I had to give, plus more I didn't know I had until the challenge was sufficient to uncover it.

MY PRAYER

When things got their darkest, when the cloud of divorce lay heavy on my mind, when I felt myself being squashed under a burden that seemed to be heavier day by day, when I felt that Nancy would die and our efforts were a waste, that's when I wrote this prayer.

Dear Lord,

Thank you for this opportunity to be part of Nancy's transition.

Whatever you need me to do, I give myself to you in order for your Will to be done.

Please grant me the strength and courage to accept events as they happen.

Please grant me the patience and clarity to be unattached.

Please help me grow beyond my desires for Nancy's peaceful passing soon.

Please help me understand and accept that your Will can give as well as take.

Please, Dear Lord, open my heart to the possibility of Nancy's recovery.

Please, Dear Lord, open my heart to the needs of others.

Please, Dear Lord, help me to remember that Thy Will is done.

Thank you for giving me this deep level of understanding.

Please continue to guide me.

Amen

THE TRANSITION—
MID-NOVEMBER 1983

The most difficult part of each day for me has become the morning. I wake up and wonder if the woman in the next room—my wife, my love—is alive or dead. We are at her mother's home in San Diego in order for Nancy to be with her family and friends and close to the hospital in Tijuana, Mexico, where she has been going over the past year. Unlike Seattle, it's warm here, and the dry air eases the stress in her lungs. She is in 'her' room, the room she had as a young girl. She is able to look out of the windows and see 'her' mountains, the mountains she has loved all of her life. She is in too much discomfort for us to share a bed. I sleep in the extra room down the hall.

I wake up, say my prayer and do my morning routines before looking in on her. I take care of my routines first so that I can freely handle any needs she may have. As I wash, I go through my doubts and wonderings, exploring possible scenarios and coming up with plans. I'm a planner; I like to be prepared for any eventuality. Anxiety comes up as I think about my job and business responsibilities back home in Seattle. I've been flying back and forth between San Diego and Seattle for the past month, balancing my responsibilities in Seattle with my love/caring/devotion to Nancy here in this more supportive environment.

It's been a week since Nancy called me to say she thinks she's dying. I took the next flight south. And what a week it has been: our discussing and making funeral arrangements,

Nancy telling me of her trips through the *bardos*,[1] her mother going through her grief in her own way, me going through mine, coordinating help, and dealing with a constant stream of visitors. (We had to stop it and give visits by appointment only; the demands of each visit wore Nancy out.) I'm thankful that we had as much help as we did. It lightened my load considerably and helped Nancy's mother keep some sort of domestic order. Still, I felt the reluctant ringmaster, keeping it all together because the others were looking to me for direction, while inside I just wanted to sit down and cry. But I kept at it. Fortunately, one of our helpers was caring enough to tell me when I was in the way and ought to go take a walk.

I look in on her as she wakes. I see her wasting away, accepting her fate, accepting the task of focusing her energy for making her transition. Yet, today she seems stronger than I've seen her for some time. We talk.

Later she surprised us all. She got out of bed, took a shower and came upstairs for her meals. She was in great spirits. She even sat outside for awhile, taking the sun. She seems a long way from death. She looks like she did several months ago, tired but vibrant. I'm relieved and happy to see her up and about and able to take care of herself unaided. In our high spirits, I completely forget about Walter's plateau. So, I decide to return to Seattle the next day in order to take care of my responsibilities there.

Two days after I return, I am fired. I am not given a reason. I can only guess that my absences and preoccupation with Nancy became more than my boss wanted to deal with. Losing this job as an apartment complex manager also means losing our residence. I am given four weeks to move. I feel betrayed.

I cried and prayed. I prayed for guidance and for relief from the increasing pressures that were bearing down on me. That evening, I went walking through the Seattle Center, where I happened upon a revival meeting. During a group prayer in which the minister called forth the power of the Holy Spirit, I

1 There is more information about the *bardos* further on in this chapter and in Appendix II.

felt a clarity which directed me to sell all of our stuff except essentials and move to San Diego.

That weekend, I held a big moving sale. Late Saturday afternoon, on the first day of the sale, I receive a phone call. Nancy is in the hospital in Tijuana. I talk with the doctor. Nancy's situation is serious. He gives her less than a week. I check my flight schedule. It's too late to catch a flight down tonight. I have dinner out with friends, then go home and go to bed. I'm exhausted, yet sleep comes reluctantly.

Sunday morning, I wake shortly before 7:30. I automatically look at the clock when I wake up. At 8:00 A.M., the telephone rings. I receive the message I had been expecting during the past weeks of shuttling back and forth. Nancy is dead.

I pack my bag, apologize to the people waiting outside to get into our moving sale and catch the next plane to San Diego. My immediate reactions are a mix of relief, sadness, shock and joy. I feel a weight lift off my shoulders. I feel the beginnings of the void known as grief opening up before me. On the plane, I talk with the person next to me about living in Northern California. I stare out the window most of the time. I don't remember landing.

During our last weeks together, Nancy related to me her experiences as she traveled through the *bardos*. The *bardos* are the levels of life and afterlife experiences as described by Tibetan Buddhism. They are: the *Bardo* of Life, the *Bardo* of the Dream State, the *Bardo* of Meditation, the *Bardo* of the Process of Death, the *Bardo* of the State after Death and the *Bardo* of the Search for Rebirth in Samsara (the cycle of becoming and passing). Nancy was a student of Tibetan Buddhism and felt comfortable with the terminology. The *bardos* relating to afterlife are analogous to the levels of Heaven and Hell in Christianity, or the realms of the gods and demigods in both Western and Eastern religions and myths.

Initially, she described the presence of an "energy-pulling body" (the angel of death?) which came to her. It moved down through her body, causing heat in her head, followed by nausea. Nancy described her physical body as "here in the solid dimension being pulled into a dimension that isn't solid." She related that she felt her body being pulled apart, as if she had two bodies—a solid body and a non-solid body—"hanging together" in this other realm. She said she felt that her physical body was changed to a "vast, empty chamber that no longer fit" her.

This reminds me of a teaching found primarily in the spiritual literature of the East and in metaphysical and some spiritual literature of the West, that we are all incarnated souls who have taken on human bodies in order to accomplish certain things or learn specific lessons, such as practicing unconditional love, in this plane of existence. When we souls have completed our mission, whether it takes 80 years or 80 hours, our bodies are dropped, discarded like articles of clothing which no longer fit, as they are no longer needed to keep us here on Earth. When a soul drops its body with no attachments to the physical realm and with complete focus of its energy on returning to be with God, that's exactly where the soul goes. A soul who doesn't want to leave or whose mind gets distracted by fear and panic during the transition process, thus blocking the clarity of energy needed to attain Oneness with the Source, ends up in the in-between places, such as purgatory and the lower levels of the spiritual realm including the ghost state. I agree with Srila Prabhupada, who taught that ghosts are soul spirits whose energy became so ensnared and entangled in attachments to this plane of existence that they hadn't enough energy left to make the entire journey upward. Thus, they are forced to hang around here until they are given an energy boost by being prayed upward by concerned, loving relatives and friends or are reincarnated in order to do death again without attachments.

After Nancy got used to being in her non-solid body, she began to relate more of her experiences in this other dimension. She spoke of being with her spiritual master and her spiritual teacher, both of whom had died fairly recently. After these meetings, Nancy always came back into her solid, physical body with an air of peace which permeated her entire being. Even though her body was in an advanced state of degeneration, her face glowed. She radiated peace, love and strength of purpose. When back in her physical body, she often announced that she was feeling stronger, was getting better and was feeling well again. My intuition was that this was her soul talking, feeling strengthened by the soul intercourse she was having with her spiritual master and teacher. My observation of her physical condition did not jibe with what she said.

It was during these initial phases of the transition process that we learned which foods are appropriate for a dying person. Those foods are liquids, fruit juices, perhaps some soft fruit or perhaps some yogurt. These light foods are ideal. Heavier foods do not fit the non-solid state of the body. Heavier solid foods cause nausea and vomiting because a person's energy is not there in the solid physical body to digest them. Vomiting itself is a strain that both detracts from and depletes a person's energy-focusing as they travel from one world into another.

Her reports were not unlike similar reports I have read in which spiritually advanced people tell of their journeys through the inner realms during deep meditation and meditation-like states. Interestingly, meditation teachers often advocate a diet of light foods, preferably vegetarian, instead of a heavier diet based on meat.

Two dear friends, Peter and Mary, were with Nancy during her final hours. They were my surrogates; they did everything I would have done. They totally supported Nancy as she made her transition. They had the advantage, though, of nonattachment, thus allowing Nancy complete freedom to focus all of her energy inward and upward. As Peter told me later, "This was the most intense spiritual experience of my life." Here is what they related to me.

Nancy was resting comfortably in her bed in the hospital. She had pictures of her loved ones on her bedside stand. She was holding a picture of her spiritual master, His Holiness Karmapa. A recording of Ram Dass chanting, *"Om mani padme hom,"* was playing softly in the background.

Only Mary, Peter and Nancy were in the room. "There are people all around me here that I don't like," Nancy said.

"Go higher," Peter responded, recognizing that she was experiencing one of the lower levels populated by souls and demigods still working through their own attachments to the material/physical plane of existence.

After awhile, Peter asked if she would like some music. "I hear music everywhere," Nancy replied. For the next hour or so, Peter and Mary sat in the stillness of the room, shifting back and forth between their meditations and caring for Nancy.

Something was said regarding the television set in the room and the impression Nancy had of seeing her spiritual master on the TV screen. Peter asked, "Do you want the TV on?"

Nancy replied, "I see Karmapa everywhere." Soon after, she took a deep breath and sighed out *"Om."* There was a pause. She took another breath and exhaled. There was a longer pause. She inhaled slowly and exhaled. Then her soul left her body. Her eyes were closed. Her face glowed. She radiated peace. She had no pain.

Mary described seeing waves of energy leaving Nancy's body at the moment of death. "It was as if a mighty wind that didn't move, a nonmoving rush of wind that was a love energy, came and swooped her up," Mary related. "A sweep of love like a mighty wind that didn't move . . . Love just swooped her up. Nancy was taken up so high and was so protected by the love energy, I felt she was taken to high temples of healing."

As we talked, Mary said, "I'd never experienced Buddha's vibration before, but when Nancy left her body, you could feel

His presence in the room. All the spiritual leaders—Jesus, Buddha, whoever—all have a loving, compassionate vibration that is pretty much the same. They're all so sweet. Yet, each has a subtle difference. Buddha has his own flavor. He's as different from the others as chocolate is different from strawberry."

Mary's voice sounded sad, relieved and excited as she finished her story. "We chanted and sang after she left her body," she said, "until there was no Nancy there, until she was gone, totally gone. Then we turned around and saw a rainbow in the sky outside her room's window."

A rainbow appearing at the time of a death is a most auspicious sign in both Tibetan Buddhism and in the Bible. In Tibetan Buddhist understanding, a rainbow signifies that a soul has returned to the Buddha Fields, to the home of the Lord Most High. In the Bible, a rainbow appearing in the heavens is a sign of the covenant between God and man.

According to Emanuel Swedenborg, the eminent 18th century Swedish scientist and theologian, a rainbow "signifies the state of the regenerate spiritual man" (*Arcana Coelestia*, n. 1042). A rainbow denotes the stage of development of a spiritually renewed or transformed person whose life is based on the truth of living from principles higher than those found in physical nature.

When I arrived at the hospital the next day, everyone was strangely subdued. It was *very* quiet. I could tell that a lot of crying had been going on from the tear-streaked faces that met me. They all loved her. "Nancy was *especial*," one nurse told me. And Nancy, who had told me several times of the remarkable, totally caring staff at the hospital, had loved all of them too.

Several months later, I met a fellow Seattleite who happened to be in the room next to Nancy's during her last hours. (There are no accidents.) He told me that he could feel the energy in the air. He said, "This lady is crossing over tonight, and she knows it." He told me that the staff at the hospital did everything they could to make her transition as comfortable as possible. He said, "They were pouring their hearts out." I believe it.

The attending physician recorded that Nancy had died at 7:30 A.M.

There are three states a person passes through after his death before arriving in heaven or hell. The first state involves his more outward aspects, the second involves his more inward aspects and the third is a state of preparation. The person passes through these states in the world of the spirits.

There are however some people who do not pass through these states, being either taken up into heaven or cast into hell immediately after death. The people who are immediately taken up into heaven are the ones who have been regenerated and thus made ready for heaven in the world. People who have been regenerated and made ready in this way need only to cast off their soiled natural elements along with their bodies and are immediately taken into heaven by angels. I have seen them taken up an hour after death.

EMANUEL SWEDENBORG (1688–1772)
HEAVEN AND HELL

GIVING A
SUPPORTIVE SEND-OFF

Emanuel Swedenborg explored the spiritual realms during his meditation practice over two hundred years ago. He followed in the footsteps of the Masters, as have others since then. Their reports of what they experienced, although couched in the different imagery and languages of cultures separated by distance and time, are all basically the same. Consequently, as I read different interpretations of what happens at death and of what we can do to aid a person's transition, I came to understand and appreciate the importance of supporting Nancy's transition instead of feeding my own sense of loss.

For the person going through their transition, dying is a fairly complex process. There are physical reactions taking place throughout one's body as various functions shut down. There is the distraction that comes from knowing that your legs no longer move, that your breathing has stopped, that your heart has stopped. There is the distraction of physical pain. Or there is the distraction of numbing painkillers which have made thought and concentration difficult. After one leaves one's body there is the often confusing awareness of knowing what is going on around you as if you were still alive, but without being able to communicate with others. Then there is the awesome experience of being vulnerably open to lights and sounds as you are thrust into a consciousness so vast that it encompasses all that is, all that was and all that is to be. For the person prepared for this adventure—the transition of the soul from its Earth/physical manifestation to pure soul essence—death becomes the most beautiful, rewarding, satisfying and wondrous experience of all. To put it another way, if you are ready to meet your Maker, you will. Such a person is, as Swedenborg records, "immediately taken into heaven by angels." I believe this is what happened with Nancy, since we were given the sign, the rainbow, which indicates, in the Buddhist tradition, that a soul has made it to heaven.

For the person who is not prepared, death is frightening, threatening, terrifying and subject to unpleasant results. While Swedenborg describes it somewhat gently as the "three states a person passes through," the Hebrew tradition calls it Gehenna, named after the garbage dump in the valley of Hinnom near old Jerusalem where fires were kept burning continually to prevent pestilence. Some souls linger in Gehenna until they figure out where they are and what has happened to them.

While part of a person's transition is going forward with trust and confidence in their spiritual understanding, the other part is letting go of the physical plane (especially the body) they are leaving. Some souls have a more difficult time of letting go of their physical bodies than do others because of their attachments to the physical plane of existence. What we, the living, do at this time can have an affect on how successful a soul is in ridding itself of its attachments.

According to the Tibetan tradition and according to the ever-increasing literature on after-death experiences as related by those who have returned from the dead, soul entities do hear as well as see what is going on in the room in which their dead body lies. Since the soul entity is aware of what takes place among those living people in the room, what the living people do has a direct influence on how fully the soul entity is released from entanglements in the physical plane. The worst possible scene for a departing soul to see would be relatives fighting over the departed person's possessions. Remember, even Ebenezer Scrooge in Dickens's *A Christmas Carol* felt the arrows of disrespect and unkindness pierce his heart as he watched his housekeeper sell his personal goods to a thief and saw his business associates' lack of concern over his death.

In contrast, a person who dies in the company of people

who support the dying person's spiritual path is experiencing an ideal situation because the soul entity sees, after leaving its body, people who are concerned for the success of the soul's journey upward. This understanding supports the significance of some form of last rites for the dying person. For Nancy, a Lama visited her in the hospital to give her last rites. According to the meditation master, the Venerable Lama Sogyal Rinpoche, "Whatever she or he believes in most is what you should affirm. If the person believes in a particular form or image of God, that is the form that will come to her or him after death."

The spiritual Master, Charan Singh, answered one of his follower's questions regarding dying by saying that one should have fellow believers in the room with the dying person and have the family and friends who are most attached in another room. By physically separating the dying person from those having strong attachments, the attachments and the people's involvement in feelings of loss will not interfere with the soul entity's efforts to extract itself from this plane of existence. I believe that my absence from Nancy's side at the moment of her transition helped her soul complete its process. I have no regrets.

I like what Jesus says in Matthew 13:44–45: "The kingdom of heaven is like treasure hidden in a field, which a man found and covered up; then in his joy he goes and sells all that he has and buys that field. Again, the kingdom of heaven is like a merchant in search of fine pearls, who, in finding one pearl of great value, went and sold all that he had and bought it." I think we can help our loved ones get to the kingdom of heaven when they die by being like the stuff sold by the people in Jesus' parables. We step aside, get out of the way, accept that our time of usefulness is past. Our loved ones can no longer afford to spend time with us baubles and trinkets now that their own pearl of great price is within reach. As difficult as it may be for some of us, we must let our loved ones die in peace and give them our total support as we encourage them onward and upward. We'll have plenty of time to work through all of our attachments to them later, during our grief process.

When the soul energy seems to need encouragement to leave this physical realm and go home to the higher, spiritual realm, the Tibetan Buddhist practice is to chant prayers into the left ear of the departed one's body. In cases of severe reluctance on the part of the soul to leave, a priest is brought in who does special, powerful prayers which, in a sense, exorcise the soul out of the body. Of course, we are all not Tibetan Buddhists. However, we can learn from their teachings and understanding of death and the dying process and apply what we learn within the practice of our own religious teachings and spiritual path. Prayers given to encourage a soul to be with Jesus, Krishna, Allah, Ram, Buddha, or Yahweh can be very helpful.

Why the left ear and not the right? According to Dr. Randolph Stone, the founder of the study of the human energy system known as Polarity Therapy, the left side of the body is the receptive side of the body. Because of the way in which electromagnetic energy flows over, around and through the human form, the left side of our bodies is more sensitive to receiving stimuli and energy inputs, while our right side is more involved with our outgoing energy. By chanting or praying into the left ear of the 'dead' body, we would be feeding into the receptive energy flow.

All of this may seem rather esoteric. But perhaps the viewing, during which we go to the body in the casket to say our private good-byes and best wishes, evolved from an ancient understanding of energy flow and the reluctance of some souls to release their attachments to the physical plane.

The Hindu tradition is more to the point. They hold that the body should be cremated before the next sundown so that the soul will not have a body in which to continue its attachment to the physical plane. The Hebrew tradition, which holds that a body should be buried in a plain wooden biodegradable coffin as soon as possible unless the day is the Sabbath, in which case the body must be buried within three days maximum, is similar in that it emphasizes getting rid of the dead body as soon as possible. The Hebrew tradition, however, bases its understanding on ancient laws of hygiene recorded in the Old Testament rather than on the concept of a soul being reluctant to leave its body. In either case, it is clear that a dead body needs to be buried or cremated very quickly. Embalming a body in order to have it around as long as possible before disposing of it seems to serve no good purpose to the deceased. Rather, it plays into the survivors' attachments, their longing to have their loved one still with them.

So, how can we deal with our attachments and get them out of the way long enough to give us the opportunity to give a supportive good-bye to our loved one who is dying?

Various teachers suggest meditating in the presence of a dying person. This allows you to be an observer, watching your thoughts and feelings as they go by without stopping to examine them, without placing values on them, without judging them and without becoming them. For example, when the feeling of sadness comes up, instead of saying to yourself, "I am sad," i.e., I am being sadness, say, "Here is sadness. It is part of my repertoire of feelings. Sadness is here and then it goes." Do this often enough, and you will see all of the thoughts and feelings that are being prompted on stage by your attachments. This technique is used not to deny the thoughts and feelings, but to see them for what they are and then put them aside for later in order to be clear, encouraging and supportive now during your last moments together.

If you are unfamiliar with meditation, perhaps you could use a system a friend of mine told me about. I used it and found that it really helped clear my mind of all the tension and anxiety I felt. I would sit at the foot of Nancy's bed in the most comfortable chair I could find. I would close my eyes and listen to my breath going in and out. At first, I had to force my mind to think "In . . . out . . . in . . . out." But after awhile, it became second nature. I could shut my eyes and listen to my breath, and my mind would think, "In . . . out . . . in . . . out," automatically. With practice, I found that this would put me in a calm, peaceful state which allowed me to relax and view the event I was involved in without becoming overwhelmed by any of the thoughts and feelings which cropped up.

Nancy appreciated my clarity, as it helped her say her good-byes. I appreciated it too. It allowed me to use the advice of the Venerable Lama Sogyal Rinpoche, who said that your good-byes to the dying person need to be given with confidence and humor.

When Nancy and I said what became our final good-byes, I said, "Consider me your Captain Cheerleader. I am cheering you upward. I am encouraging you to leave completely this realm of existence. Don't stay here for my sake. Go as high and as far as you can. Be with God. I love you, Nancy. Go, Team, Go!!"

THE BLESSING
OF THE DEAD

The attendant at the Mexican funeral home was very kind. Although he spoke no English, he knew the language of the heart. His eyes conveyed sympathy, compassion and the desire to be of service. He discreetly withdrew from the room as I approached Nancy's body.

Seeing her physical form lying on the wheeled carrier, I reflected on when I had last seen her alive and when I had first seen her. Those mental images are with me still. I brushed a few stray hairs from her face and bent over her for one last look. I had no intention of kissing her. I did not want to touch her. As a tactilely oriented person, I remember through my hands. I wanted my tactile memory of her to be warm and alive.

As I bent over her, my face directly over hers, about six inches away, I felt this zap, like the electrical discharge of a capacitor, hit me right between the eyes in the area of my 'third eye' in the lower center of my forehead. My third eye felt warm, as in the warmth of a good feeling.

Later, several months later, while sharing this experience with Ram Dass, he said that I had received the blessing of the dead. He told me that his guru had once told him about the blessing of the dead, that it is the highest blessing a person can receive and that the person who receives one is indeed fortunate. He said that I was very fortunate to receive this blessing.

I have since come to the conclusion that what I had received was the last big charge of Nancy's soul energy transmitting itself from her body's psychic center to mine. It's a loving way of saying good-bye. It is also the most precious gift someone can give to another. In spite of all my earlier entreaties to her to focus all of her energy inward and upward for her soul's journey back to the Source, she kept a little behind to give to me. Knowing Nancy, I'm sure she did it on purpose.

Recently I shared this experience with a group of friends. One woman responded that she had had a similar experience when she paid her last respects to her dead grandmother. She said that as she got close to her grandmother, she felt something hit her between the eyes, something like a warm, buzzing sensation. She didn't tell anyone about it. She thought maybe there was something wrong with her from the stress and strain of the event. She was relieved to learn her experience was real, not imagined, and that it was a blessing from her grandmother to her, the blessing of the dead.

FRIENDS AND RELATIONS

Soon after Nancy died, I flew back to my familial home in Delaware. I stayed with my parents for several months while going through the shock that immediately follows the death of a loved one. I felt a hole in my life. I experienced the real physical pain of heartache. I spent hours sitting on the edge of the bed, staring at the wall. I would get in my brother's VW, which he so generously lent me, and drive all over the place with little idea as to where I was going, where I had been or why I was doing it. Very often I would return at the end of a day's drive and have no idea of where I had gone. I put 4,000 miles on his car in three months. Outside of a few specific destinations, I went nowhere in particular. It seems the driving gave me something to do. Besides, being on the move made it unnecessary to interact with other people, which I was having difficulty doing anyway.

In my mother's library, I found a book on the domestic life of Thomas Jefferson. Among other personal accounts, it records his reactions to his wife's death early in their marriage. According to his niece, Jefferson locked himself in his room at Monticello and paced back and forth day and night, until he would collapse on his couch and sleep. He did this for three weeks. He then called for his horse and took long rides all over. No one knew where he went or how long he would be gone. He didn't seem to know either. After reading this account, I felt in good historical company on my long, seemingly aimless drives.

Christmas was awkward. My parents and brother opened gifts Nancy and I had gotten for them on an earlier trip to Mexico. They did really well, considering the situation. However, I was in shock. I may have been participating on the outside, but inside I was somewhere else. Inside, I felt I was suspended in the center of a vast, empty space. I felt helpless, both from a lack of inner motivation and from an inability to be complete in my interactions with the rest of the world. To paraphrase Rocky Balboa, I was in my gaps.

My mother was especially affected by Nancy's death. She had been so happy when I finally married. (I was 39.) Now, the daughter she had always wanted was dead of cancer, the same disease which had taken her sister and had caused her to lose a breast twenty years ago. We didn't talk much about it, but I could feel her sorrow every time I looked at her.

My father and I didn't talk much about it either. We never talked much about things anyway. He put his feelings into his music, to which he has devoted his entire life. He's an excellent musician, and I always enjoy hearing him play. He played his accordion and sang two of his own compositions at our wedding. We would not have wanted it any other way. I know Nancy's death has hurt him. I wish I knew how. Perhaps he said it, and I didn't hear.

My brother and I communicate very well. We share the same spiritual understanding and the same appreciation for what our parents have given us. Although we have not followed the parental admonition to settle down and get steady, i.e., regular, jobs, we are living our own lives, just as our parents are living theirs. He was my best man. Being with my brother on long walks through Manhattan (where he is an actor) was very comforting. At one point we stopped for a moment, and he said, "I really don't know what you're going through, but I do know what you're going through."

What he said sums up what most of my friends and relatives were able to convey. We sympathize with you, but we really have no idea as to the extent of what you are feeling. They had good intentions, for which I'm grateful, but their expressions were not always helpful. The worst were those who tried to cheer me up. In effect, they were discounting my grief and pain, which is not what I needed. I needed them to recognize that I was hurting badly, so badly that I was not always able to express what I needed. Consequently, I tended to react defensively. Shock coupled with the feeling of treading on a fragile bridge over the deep chasm of the unknown tended to make me act first and think after.

Ultimately, I found myself alone in my grief. And it was much, much more intense than any grief I had ever before experienced. I began to question what was happening to me. Was this the grief one goes through when a loved one dies? Or was this "old stuff," taking advantage of the situation, coming back to drag me through it again? Or both? Shouldn't I be wearing black instead of buying a turquoise sport shirt? Was I doing grief correctly?

I needed someone to be an indicator, a guide to the way to do grief. I needed someone who had also recently experienced the death of a loved one, someone who I felt would understand my questions and actions.

I visited a relative whose husband had died a year before. I hoped that she would help me get my bearings. In the few short hours we spent together, I learned that the event had not altered her basic personality. If anything, she was even more feisty and uniquely individualistic. But when it came to the nitty-gritty of the grief process (for example, what to do with the spouse's things), she was dealing with it by not dealing with it. Contrary to my way of diving in, sorting out and eliminating, she was closing the doors on rooms full of his things with the idea of sometime (in the future) getting an appraiser and maybe selling some things. She refused my offer of help and showed no interest in my questions about certain items.

She taught me by example that each of us does grief in our own way. There is no correct way and there is no wrong way to go through the grief process. There is only the process itself; and at all times we are making decisions as to which way we want to go with it. We choose to hang on here or let go there, to cry in public or to hold it in until we have our privacy, to continue our daily routine or to take some time off. Whatever we choose to do or express, we choose it because it seems right for us at that moment.

One day while reading the newspaper, I saw an announcement for a meeting of a group of widows and widowers who are young and active, like myself. I went. It was wonderful. Here was a group with which I could relate. We were, all of us, actively participating in the world through raising families and/or pursuing our careers. And we all had lost our spouses. Here was the reflection I needed, the opportunity to share with peers this tumultuous event in my life.

At the meeting I met a woman who sounded as if her husband had died only yesterday. She was grieving and upset and didn't know what to do. It turned out he had died over two and a half years before. Another woman, a young woman only 26 years old, had lost her husband after 11 months of marriage. She was relieved to find that yet another woman hadn't taken her husband's pants off the hook on the closet door either. There was a fellow who was facing the challenge of raising four children while maintaining his full-time job. I met people from all walks of life who were dealing with the problems of daily living while going through the life-opening experience of the death of a spouse. Each one was doing it in his or her own way. Many were relieved to find that others shared the same questions, feelings and problems. And I was happy to get the reflection I needed. I was doing all right. My way of dealing with grief was validated. We each go through the same process, but we do it in our own unique way. There is no right way; there is no wrong way. There is only the opportunity to open one's self to the experience and learn from it, transcend it or be smothered by it—all within the realm of one's own choosing. To paraphrase an American Indian expression, the grief process is a great place to learn or to die.

My hope is that I am learning something from all this and that I will not be smothered by it. My relief comes in knowing that the means I use to realize my hope are not all that important. Even though I've gotten hung up on the details, the ways in which I am going through my grief, they really don't matter.

Whatever I do is all right, provided of course that I am maintaining myself as a socially responsible person. What matters is the outcome.

1984

THE PHASES OF GRIEF

Psychologists and researchers have observed many different people who were going through their grief. Here is a summary of their observations.

The grief process consists of phases, during which there are evident behavioral changes. Even though there are similarities, no two people experience grief in exactly the same way. Also, the lengths of time spent in the grief process are often quite different. Judging one's own grief behavior against the behavior of others frequently causes doubt and/or confusion.

The following are some of the behavioral changes people experience during the grief process:

PHASE I	PHASE II	PHASE III
Shock	Frustration	Gradual recovery
Numbness	Loneliness	Feeling better physically
	Emotional release/outburst	Low periods less often
	Anger	Acceptance
	Guilt	Adjustment
	Denial	Remembering more realistically
	Panic	Experimenting with new activities
	Inability to be logical	Creativity in living
	Symptoms of physical illness	Normalization of relationships
	Depression	Commitment to others
	Reclusiveness	
	Crazy feelings	
	Bizarre behavior	
	Difficulty with normal relationships	

A SAD DAY—
SEATTLE—SPRING 1984

In grieving, I have come to a low point in my life. Not that the grieving has brought me down. Grieving is a positive process. Grief is the emptying out of all those feelings. It's just that while all this grief is going on, the rest of my life also feels stymied. My one main focus now is writing down this experience. I guess it's a way of finding meaning in this sea of perplexity.

My life support system feels so precarious. I'm having unbelievably bad luck in finding a place to live. Those few places I've been offered are either too physically small or are psychologically cramping. For example, as much as my friends, Karl and Laurie, wanted me to share their house with them, I could not accept their offer. Seeing their loving-couple energy so soon after the loss of my wife was more than I could handle. The places I've wanted to move into I haven't been getting. Now I waver between being open to what is offered and accepting it no matter what, or toughing it out and getting exactly what I want, or accepting the closed doors as a sign from the universe to forget Seattle and move somewhere else. This continuing frustration regarding a place to live is upsetting of itself. To have it complexified by my going through the loss of my wife really gets to me at times.

I'm feeling a lot of disappointment with my life. I feel at a standstill. I obviously need to do something, make some move that will reduce the pressure and allow me to do the paperwork I need to do to rebuild my life and to get focused on what I want to be doing five years from now. Maybe that's why I dream of travel, including moving back to the East Coast. That would certainly keep my life busy for a while.

I feel a lack of joy in my life. I feel sad. I miss Nancy. I miss my brother.

Nancy, I really miss you.

ANGER

Why her? Why him? Why me? Why now?

When Nancy died, I felt angry and frustrated. Suddenly, the object of all my energy, attention and resources was no longer there. I was running full tilt, mobilized as if for a war, focusing everything on supporting Nancy. When she died, I felt frustrated by the vacuum I faced. There is no glory in cleaning up the debris of warfare. It takes as much energy, but the reason is quite unclear. I needed to once again remind myself to trust in the Lord, do the best possible job and accept that what is happening now is merely a step on the way to what happens next.

However, those reminders did not stop my feelings of frustration; they were still there. But it did take the edge off so that even though I still felt frustration while sorting through the debris of a three-year battle with cancer, the frustration was not immobilizing. I recognized my feeling, watched my frustration without becoming it and went on about my business.

My anger, however, was something else. I felt anger toward the various cancer research institutions I had contacted within the United States. None had offered any direct help. At best, they referred me to another organization. Yet every few months I had read of another cancer "breakthrough," with a possible cure on the horizon. Those tantalizing news stories promised much and delivered little. And this has been going on for years. Obviously, I thought in my anger, there is no money in actually finding a cure, but there is lots of money to be made in looking. My anger with these organizations was that when I needed them, they offered no help. I felt abandoned and let down by their empty promises.

In talking with others who have lost loved ones to different causes, I found a common thread of anger running through our conversations. Practically everyone was angry with their spouse for dying. Very few shared my anger with the national organizations. Some were angry with the doctors. One friend was candid in sharing with me her anger toward her now dead husband. As she put it, "I was mad at him for leaving me. I felt abandoned [by him]." She called this her "little girl syndrome"—wanting to be taken care of. Her feeling of being abandoned led to a feeling of personal rejection, having been rejected by the one who died. In defense, she got angry with him for leaving her. As she put it, "If he really loved me, why did he leave me?"

In that statement is the expression of resentment toward the person who died for having abandoned the living lover. Resentment is the glowing ember which rekindles old anger. Thus, we have (1) the feeling of having been abandoned by the one who died, leading to (2) the feeling of having been rejected because the person left them, leading to (3) resentment toward the person for dying. This resentment expresses itself as anger at the person for "having done this to me" (they went and died), and anger at God for taking away the loved one and "having done this to me."

My deeper personal anger, one shared by another newly widowed and also by a man who had lost his only son, was my anger over frustrated expectations. When Nancy and I married, we had dreams, plans, expectations of what our future would be. We dedicated ourselves to building this future together. Her death left me with a handful of suddenly meaningless blueprints. Her death left me with plans and expectations which were now no longer based on reality.

I got angry when she died, angry at her cancer for taking her away, angry at her cancer for destroying our plans and my hopes and expectations, and angry at her cancer for taking, taking, taking—taking her life, taking our love, taking my lover, taking our resources—and giving nothing in return. I dealt with my anger by sublimating it into work. I took all my anger energy and put it into what I called Broom Therapy. I would sweep—sweep the sidewalks, sweep the gutters, sweep cobwebs, real and imagined, off the walls. I have become quite proficient in the use of a broom.

In sharing my anger with my friend with the "little girl syndrome," she said, "You're not angry with Nancy?"

"No."

"You're angry with her cancer?"

"Yes."

"Well, I was angry with my husband. The way I finally got over my anger was to forgive him for dying."

Forgive. The way to get over one's anger at another is to forgive. "Forgive us our trespasses as we forgive those who trespass against us." She forgave her husband for dying, which also meant her coming to grips with and releasing her feelings of personal rejection and abandonment. It took some doing on my part, but I finally forgave Nancy's cancer for having erased my slate full of expectations. I had to first come to grips with (recognize) and then let go of my expectations and attachments to them. As a consequence of my forgiving her cancer for what it did, I now have a clean slate with which to begin again.

How do we forgive? When I first thought about how to forgive Nancy's cancer for taking her away, my anger got in the way. I sarcastically said, "If I say, 'I forgive you,' will that really do anything?" The answer was a loud and clear "NO," since my heart wasn't in it. Eventually, after reading several essays on forgiveness, I learned that the way to forgiveness is by accepting that things are the way they are, that they will continue to be the way they are, that there is nothing I can do to control the way things are, that by forgiving things for being the way they are, I don't overtly change the outside events, but I sure affect the way in which I perceive them. In other words, to forgive is to accept. By accepting outside events, we are freed to build on the good that appears in any given situation, thus creating change in the way things are.

After forgiving the other for dying and after forgiving God for having taken the significant other, we have this incredible opportunity to take all that energy we'd been putting into being angry and redirecting it into the flip side of anger—enthusiasm. For my friend, her enthusiasm manifests in church activities. For me, my enthusiasm got these thoughts into your hands. For others who have forgiven their loved ones for dying, their anger has turned into enthusiasm which has propelled them into new careers, new relationships, travel or whole new lives.

So, to deal with your anger at the death of a loved one, (1) accept that you have anger. We all go through this, so there's really no use in trying to deny or hide your anger. If you do, it will just come out in other ways, like indigestion, liver problems, headaches, etc. (2) Observe your anger without getting caught up in it. This will let you learn how it works and how it is generated. Anger is only one in the repertoire of emotions we humans are given to use to keep body and soul together harmoniously. You are not your anger, nor is your anger the totality of your means of expression. (3) Forgive the other for dying, for destroying your plans, for frustrating your expectations, for leaving you alone, for abandoning you, etc. (4) Forgive yourself for having anger. As in other things, repression born of lack of understanding breeds misuse. (5) Redirect your anger energy into enthusiasm because (6) out of enthusiasm (for life, for a project, for a career, for a relationship) comes love. As you know, now is the time we need love the most. And the best way to get love is to give love.

What is love? Unqualified acceptance.

GUILT

Several people I've come in contact with recently who have lost loved ones have expressed their feelings of guilt over having not done enough for their loved ones while they were still alive. Often these people would say, "If only I had done such-and-such, then . . ." or "If only we had gone to Hospital X, then my husband would still be alive." I would listen to them and try to be supportive, yet there was something about what they were saying that didn't ring true with my experience. But it got so that I was beginning to think maybe I was wrong for not having such feelings. So I decided to discuss it with my teacher.

"Well," he said, urging me to continue, "what else do you think about these 'if onlys'?"

"It seems to me," I said, "the 'if onlys' presume there is something that we can do which will stop death from taking place. We may be able to duplicate and maintain physical function with our technology, but when a soul leaves its body for good, it's all for naught. When a person's spirit/soul/life essence leaves, the person dies, no matter how much we want them to still be alive. I did everything I could for Nancy. We left no stone unturned in supporting her choice of treatments for her cancer. Still, she died. Sure, there are times when I think we might have fine-tuned a method a bit more, but we were going with the information we had at a rate which we could afford in terms of time, energy and money. I don't see why I should have any guilt for not having done enough. We did all we could do."

"I understand," my teacher said. "And I hear in your voice

you needing to be reassured that what you did was right. Right?"

"Right," I answered. I felt a lump forming in my throat. My teacher always knows what's going on with me, even when he doesn't say something about it. When he does, I feel freed, allowed to open my heart to him. That's when I realize the point of all his teachings: to be a man who uses his mind to provide service which is motivated by the compassion he finds in his heart.

"All that matters," he said, "in what you do is that you do it with unconditional love. All that you do, be it a lot or a little, works only if you give it with no conditions."

I thought about what he said and asked, "Well, I thought I did that with Nancy. Still, she died."

"The rest of giving and doing with unconditional love is to accept the results—no matter what they are. Jesus gave unconditional love, and he was murdered. You gave unconditional love to Nancy, and she died. I give unconditional love to you, and sometimes I wonder if you heard anything I said," he laughed. "My point is, don't worry, be happy."

"Yes, but what about guilt?" I asked.

"Guilt," he began, "is a mind game. Guilt is a learned mental activity. Guilt is the word we use to describe our awareness of having done something 'wrong,' without recognizing our sense of responsibility as to what would have been 'right.' Guilt is based on the idea that *if you don't do* such-and-such or perform a certain way, *then* something (usually bad) will happen to you. Often accompanying the guilt thoughts are guilt feelings—self-inflicted physical manifestations of stress which make us feel as badly as we think we are.

"Guilt is also an ego trip. Guilt is the word we use to say that 'only I can feel this way for having done or not done whatever.' Guilt allows us to wallow in our own unique misery. Guilt exists in the mind of the person who thinks he or she has it and nowhere else. Guilt is not a shared activity.

"Guilt is what we learn instead of learning to be responsible for who we are and what we do. Responsibility is accountability. It is being answerable for our thoughts and actions and how they affect others. Guilt teaches us how to behave after the fact; responsibility teaches us how to live before the fact. By learning how to do guilt, instead of learning to be loving beings who are accountable for our own lives and our own actions and the results of our actions, we become perpetrators of irresponsibility. Perhaps by teaching guilt instead of teaching responsibility we are contributing to the increasing levels of crime.

"Guilt has its historical roots in our Judaeo-Christian culture, which has chosen to interpret the Ten Commandments as the Ten Do Nots, instead of as the Ten Permissions. [Please see Appendix I.] In order to enforce the Ten Do Nots, man created at least another million laws. When these didn't work either, man created the concept called guilt. For guilt to work, one must be well educated in fear and its many forms. Learning guilt instead of learning responsibility makes us vulnerable to fear. The ultimate fear, of course, is of a wrathful, destructive deity. If one believes that God, the ultimate power Whose magnitude even the mind of man cannot comprehend, is something to fear, then life can be rather scary. If, on the other hand, one takes the words of Jesus and believes that God is Love, then the burden of life is lifted, since one no longer fears the arbitrary acts of a vengeful God who deliberately seeks to destroy His Creation." He looked at me as if to say, "Don't you agree?"

"Guilt and conscience are opposites," he continued. "Guilt is acted out by being irresponsible and by groveling. Conscience is acted out by being responsible, accountable to yourself and to your fellow living beings. Conscience is the inner reminder to love and respect yourself and others. As Jiminy Cricket says, 'Always let your conscience be your guide.' Conscience is the Golden Rule: love thy neighbor as thyself. This means that in order to love and respect someone else, you first have to love and respect yourself. By first loving, honoring and respecting yourself, it is much easier to love, honor, respect and accept others, not the other way around. By first conquering your own inner demons and dragons of prejudice, lust,

greed, hate, pettiness, etc., in order to release your inner innocent love, you are in a much stronger position in which to help
others do the same thing. In a sense, the story of Saint George
and the dragon and the fair damsel becomes the story of each
one of us as we struggle to overcome our own negativities in
order to release our all-accepting, unconditional, innocent love.

"This process of being responsible to ourselves, to others
and to the gift we call life, takes effort and conscientiously applied skill and stamina. I like to call this process 'enlightened
self-interest.' It is a way of thanking Life for being alive by giving back to it. Enlightened self-interest requires my knowing
what I have to give and how to give what I have in the most
quality-effective manner. In this way, I am releasing 'the fair
damsel' within me in order to act from the feeling of loving
trust and to blend with the flow of life. The freedom that comes
with this sense of balance feels so good, especially after I've
been clanking around in my armor and swinging my sword for
such a long time.

"On the other hand, selfishness, like self-centeredness (the
dragon), places importance only on one's self (as in ego, one's
concept of one's self as manufactured by the mind, taking one's
uniqueness seriously). In selfishness, there is no real importance and certainly no equality given to other living beings.
Selfishness sends you in to slay others' dragons first because
you know what they need/should do, even though you haven't
yet done it for yourself. Selfishness also lets you use guilt as a
way out of your irresponsibility towards yourself and others,
especially when your involvements make things worse instead
of better.

"One outgrows one's need for guilt the moment one outgrows one's need to be told what not to do. It's that magic moment when the potentials of the universe open up before you,
while at the same time you recognize that the potentials of the
universe have also opened for the person next to you, even the
person sitting next to you on the bus. This is the moment when
you realize that the possibilities that come from living a life of
peace, respect and love are much greater than those possibili-

ties offered by war, arrogance and hate. The foundation of this awareness is the acceptance of responsibility for one's own actions. When this is done, laws that define 'do nots' no longer become a fence confining one's growth (and sometimes getting jumped or broken in the process). Rather, the laws become more like trees on the horizon—gentle reminders of limits—without becoming limitations in themselves.

"Well, I really got going on that one," my teacher said. "As you can see, I really believe that guilt is a non-reality being used to cover a multitude of other feelings regarding acknowledgement of one's own sense of irresponsibility."

"What if a person is guilty of a crime?" I asked.

"Guilty is just a word that denotes the person's irresponsibility," he answered. "Guilt and guilty are words that came out of our ego-minds, where 'guilt' was created in the first place. God made man innocent and loving, guiltless, if you will. Man made guilt to rationalize his decision to follow his own mind instead of flowing with the mind of God."

He looked at his clock. "My, it's late. I have to get downtown. Come back again."

"Good-bye," I said, "and thank you," as he shooed me out the door.

I thought of what my teacher said and began applying it to my life. First, I applied it to my observations of how a widow friend was acting over the death of her husband. She was not at the hospital the day he died. For weeks after his death, she went on about how guilty she felt for not being there when he died. She poured out her guilt and sought consolation from whomever would listen. "I feel so bad that I wasn't there when he died. I feel so guilty and ashamed for not being there when he died," she would say. As it turned out, she was using guilt as camouflage to hide what was really going on in her. Her true feelings were that she was afraid others would judge her harshly for taking that particular day off to rest from her total exhaustion. Thus, she judged herself by what she perceived others' standards to be, and then proceeded to punish herself by groveling around in guilt and holding in her true feelings which needed to be released. She was being irresponsible to herself and dishonest with others. So, she covered it up by being guilty. What a misery-causing choice.

The other day, I was stopped for speeding. At one level, I had broken the law. At another level, I recognized that I was being irresponsible toward the people who lived along that particular stretch of road by driving my car at a rate of speed that was potentially hazardous to them. Now I drive slower, not out of fear of getting caught, but out of respect for the people who live along the roadway. Instead of feeling guilt for a past action, I feel responsible for what I am doing now as I drive along the road.

As my teacher would say, "Guilt is an ego trip. Take the 'u' out of guilt, and you have gilt. Gilt is a thin layer of gold which not only takes on the contours of that which it covers, like skin, but also reflects the Light."

As I was growing up, I thought that I was learning to act responsibly. I did what was expected by my parents, family, school, church and society. Yet, I was beginning to have my doubts, as if I thought I was doing right, but not quite. I felt as if my actions were proper, but my inner motivation was someone else's, not my own. One day, I happened across a copy of *The Book of Mirdad* by Mikhail Naimy in a friend's kitchen, of all places. I flipped through it and stopped where, in a sense, I felt guided to stop. I read what was on the page. I felt a deep sense of release sweep through me as I found the words I needed to guide me in establishing my inner motivation for responsible action. I asked for a pencil and piece of paper and copied the following words:

> Mirdad said, "This is the way to freedom from care and pain:
> "So think as if your every thought were to be etched in fire upon the sky for all and everything to see. For so, in truth, it is.
> "So speak as if the world entire were but a single ear intent on hearing what you say. And so, in truth, it is.
> "So do as if your every deed were to recoil upon your heads. And so, in truth, it does.

"So wish as if you were the wish. And so, in truth, you are.
"So live as if your God Himself had need of you His life to live.
And so, in truth, He does."

Recently, I heard Elisabeth Kubler-Ross explain that as a person enters into the second stage (of three) of death, i.e., after the physical body has ceased to function and the soul/consciousness is making its transition into the spiritual realms, the person's consciousness becomes aware of everything, all that is taking place around it and all that it has ever thought and done. Emanuel Swedenborg observed parallel activity almost three hundred years ago. In his book, *Heaven and Hell,* he wrote, "When in this second state spirits become visibly just what they had been in themselves while in the world, what they then did and said secretly being now made manifest; for they are now restrained by no outward considerations, and therefore what they have said and done secretly they now say and endeavor to do openly, having no longer any fear of loss of reputation, such as they had in the world. They are also brought into many states of their evils, that what they are may be evident to angels and good spirits. Thus are hidden things laid open and secret things uncovered, in accordance with the Lord's words." Here Swedenborg quotes Jesus, as recorded in the Gospel of Luke, Chapter 12. "There is nothing covered up that shall not be revealed, and hid that shall not be known . . . Whatever ye have said in the darkness shall be heard in the light and what ye have spoken in the ear in the inner chambers shall be proclaimed on the housetops."

Clearly, when we practice Jesus' and Mirdad's teaching every moment of every single day, we will be so involved in being responsible for what we think, say and do that there will be very little time and even less need for guilt. That's my goal each and every day, a goal I surprise myself by attaining more often than not. It's a lot of work being conscious of everything I do and say, but it's so worth the effort. It makes it possible for me to dance in the light of life, instead of through a glass darkly.

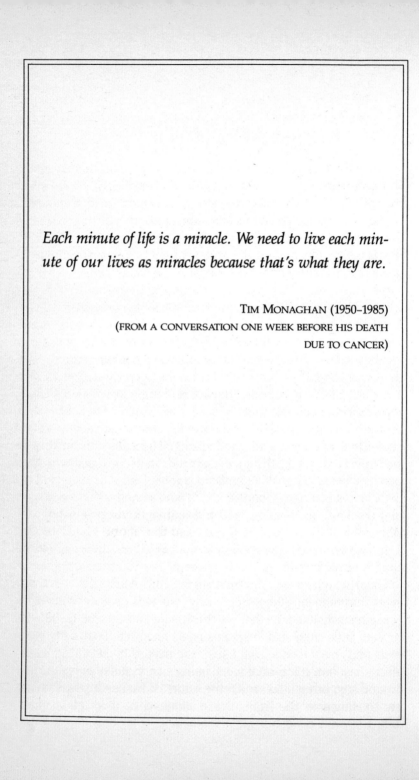

Each minute of life is a miracle. We need to live each minute of our lives as miracles because that's what they are.

TIM MONAGHAN (1950–1985)
(FROM A CONVERSATION ONE WEEK BEFORE HIS DEATH
DUE TO CANCER)

ONE DAY AT A TIME

I learned many things from Nancy as she approached death. The first lesson I learned is the importance of living one day at a time. She often said that life is a gift, that life is too precious to waste. On a less philosophical basis, we found so much going on in our lives each day that there really was not enough time to think about how we would do things a day, a week or a month away. She was completely involved in the demanding routine of her health maintenance program. I was involved in my job and business responsibilities. And we were involved with each other, not only as husband and wife, but also as care-giver and care-receiver. We lived one day at a time, not by choice, but by necessity.

Living one day at a time lovingly and responsibly is a way in which we can apply Mirdad's teaching. Living one day at a time to its fullest is also a way to avoid the "if onlys." Living one day at a time in total unconditional love can banish the "if onlys." It isn't easy, yet it is possible. More and more people are doing it every day. It's especially nice to put into practice unconditional love for another while you are together. If it's after the fact and your loved one is dead, don't fret about it. Instead, put all your good intentions to work for others you live, work and play with today.

It's also very important to remember that "if onlys" apply not only to others, but to ourselves as well. That means giving up fretting over the fish that got away or the stock or automobile I should have bought, but didn't. It means doing those things that satisfy you in a positive, uplifting way. It means using the power of positive thinking. Thank you, Norman Vincent Peale.

Fill each day with activity according to your abilities. Set a personal goal of learning at least one new thing each day, be it a word, a name, a language, a concept, an activity or something going on around you that you weren't aware of before. Explore your community, your country, your planet. That's what I strive to do, and I find it makes life very exciting. I encourage you to fill each day with your own personal meaning. Share joys. Share fears. Share feelings. Share love. Plan for tomorrow, but do for *today*. Live each and every day like it is your last day on Earth, and do it cleanly and responsibly because it just might be your last day on Earth.

THE DIFFICULTY OF LIVING ONE DAY AT A TIME IN A FUTURE-ORIENTED SOCIETY

Well-meaning friends are always asking, "What are your plans?" If I had a dollar for every time someone asked me that, I'd be very rich, indeed. The truth is I never know what to say. To even consider answering the question means getting beyond my need for being accepted for what I am right now. It's as if the well-meaning friend is saying, "The last time I saw you, you were with your spouse, and I can accept that at face value. Now your spouse is dead, and I can't relate to that. So, I need to know how you plan to reintegrate into the society of which I am a part." That question closes me down, puts me in a box and pushes me away from someone I almost desperately need to continue relating with.

For self-defense, I've come up with an answer that I hear myself repeating automatically. Then I find an excuse to remove myself from the conversation and look for someone who I hope will ask me how I feel *today*.

To help go through my grief over the death of my wife, I've found it necessary to keep my attention in the here and now. Writing this book helps me do that. I suspect that having a stable job would help too. As it is, when I'm pulled from the *now* and thrown into the *future*, it unsettles my mind from its concentration on the *present*, a present in which I feel good. When I'm forced into the future to elaborate on plans which I don't have (other than some vague notions about what I would do if I were President), my mind reacts by thinking, "I have no plans;

I have no future; I can't answer that question; I am no good."
In that state of low self-esteem, I become sensitive to my emotional vulnerability. So, I withdraw into the *past*, where I am greeted by memories of a loved one who is no longer here to share love with, which leads to feelings of being alone and lonely. Finally, I recognize that being caught up in the emptiness caused by dwelling on the past does not contribute to my feeling good about myself right now. So, I bring my mind back to the present.

In the present, I realize that (1) I do not feel good about myself because of my current lack of plans for the future; (2) I do not feel good about myself because in the past, I—with my spouse—was complete; alone, I'm incomplete; (3) I do not feel good about myself for having allowed myself to take this pinball machine route through my mind which destroyed the good self-esteem I had before I was asked, "What are your plans?"

To protect myself, I've thought of carrying a sign which says, "Don't Ask Me About My Plans." However, that's a tad ludicrous. A more sophisticated way would be to say, "I'm thinking of moving to Borneo," which would start us talking about Borneo, thus moving the conversation completely away from what I'm going through these days. After a few conversations in which I found out how little I know about Borneo, I've learned to answer *the* question with, "I'm working on a book about what I've been going through for the past several months."

Although this answer will not work for everyone who has lost a loved one or spouse (unless it happens to be true that you are writing a book), it does contain the universal seed that keeps heart and mind flowing together in the now. The seed that does this is the first word, *I'm*—that is, *I am*. *I am* is a very powerful statement of one's being in the now. There is no future; there is no past; there is only the present in the statement *I am*.

I am is a positive statement of my being in the now. "I am writing a book," also covers the future even though it states what is now, just as do the statements, "I am looking for work," or "I am looking for a place to live" (both of which are true). It seems that the more I do now in the present, the more real my future becomes. As Jesus says, "Therefore do not be anxious about tomorrow, for tomorrow will be anxious for itself. Let the day's own trouble be sufficient for the day."

In our contemporary society, which places a premium on the technological innovations of tomorrow no matter what the human, material and ecological costs for today, all of our thinking is both subtly and overtly geared toward living in the future. The economic concept of credit presumes that today's productivity has not enough value, but tomorrow's or next year's productivity will. IRAs and Keoghs create an income for the future no matter how much they disrupt governmental revenue planning today. Even diet plans promise a new you tomorrow while subtly discounting the worth of who you are today. The general thinking of our culture seems to be: today isn't good enough, but tomorrow—watch out. It's easy to fantasize a future in order to avoid living in the present.

All of this tells us that no matter who we are or what our accomplishments are today, we and our accomplishments are not good enough. This is hardly the stuff on which to feed good self-esteem. Consequently, our society is full of people who are either afraid to live in the present or don't know how or both. In our society, the future is what we live for. We have even twisted religious teachings to the point where we think that it doesn't matter what we do today, for tomorrow we will be forgiven. This line of thinking is being used to justify excesses at all levels.

In a society which lives in tomorrow, a person who lives in today appears to be going against the tide. In the greater reality, a person who lives in today, a person who goes with the flow of the moment by being completely in the moment, is going with the tide. As the great Chinese sage, Lao Tzu, says, "Those who flow as life flows know they need no other force: They feel no wear, they feel no tear, they need no mending, no repair."

Consider a person who finds he has a catastrophic illness.

What is his future? Suffering and death, hardly something to look forward to. Many people in this situation consume all sorts of drugs (both legal and illegal) in order to make themselves numb to the experience they are involved in until it is over. Others accept their situation, and instead of rejecting it, they do all they can do each day, one day at a time. They make each minute count. They live in the miracle of life minute by minute. An example of this is the now-paralyzed artist who draws pictures with a pencil she holds in her teeth.

Then there is the increasing number of retired people who, because they have no ability to live in the present, die before their seventieth year. They had spent all of their lives building for tomorrow, for their retirement. Tomorrow arrives, becomes the here and now, and they don't know what to do.

Living in the present, no matter what your age or situation, means filling your waking hours with constructive activity, doing all those things that need doing now and doing them so that they get done. There is no room for procrastination in living in the present. There is only room for focused concentration on what is happening right now, be it painting a rusting wheelbarrow, watching pigeons courting, designing a bridge or counting stars.

A friend shared with me appreciation for how I was doing in my grief. He said, "I admire how you're keeping busy, taking care of yourself and putting your life back together. What's your secret?" I thanked him and told him that I have no plans other than taking care of the things that need to be taken care of and being open to whatever happens. It's like playing a game; you take advantage of the opportunities that present themselves and accept your losses as part of the game, all the time knowing that as long as you're on the board, you're still in the game. I also use prayer at the end of the day as a welcome and relaxing way to review each day's accomplishments with God. This allows me to reflect on how I spent my time, and, as Gandhi says, "Prayer is the key of the morning and the bolt of the evening."

My friend said, "You must have some plans."

I responded clearly and without any feelings of having been invalidated, "I do. My plan is to find a place to live, find a job, sort through the boxes of stuff (both Nancy's and mine), keep what is relevant to my life today, discard the rest, and write and publish this book."

Then we discussed his upcoming marriage.

SHARING

The second lesson I received from this experience is to share with the dying person—share everything. Nancy's visitors (and visitors of other dying people I've had the opportunity to be with) tended to come in two categories: those who openly shared their feelings and those who didn't. Those who did share spoke freely with Nancy about what they were going through in regards to their feelings about Nancy and her situation. There were a lot of happy/sad tears on those occasions, happy that they were openly sharing their love and concern for each other, and sad that they were saying good-bye to each other. Notice, I said "each other." When a visiting friend openly shared with Nancy what he or she was feeling, it gave Nancy a chance to open up and freely share what she was experiencing. Thus, in sharing openly, two, three, four or more people at a time learned what it is like to be dying while giving of themselves in a way that kept Nancy very much in the here and now.

On the other hand, those who didn't share their feelings tended to arrive "all smiles," using a limited vocabulary based on the phrase "Get well soon." Although they were well-intentioned, their approach, which was basically an act, tended to put Nancy on a shelf. By their not responding to the reality of Nancy's dying, or perhaps choosing to respond with this non-involving approach, they did not experience the release which comes from crying with the one who is leaving. Instead, they cried somewhere else. The non-sharers also deprived themselves of knowing what is really going on. For Nancy, sitting through these visits was trying and tiring. She knew their pain, yet they insisted on compounding it by putting on an act. It hurt her to know that they were not being honest with her. When I later asked some of them why they didn't share their sorrow with Nancy, they said that they didn't want to hurt her feelings. Because of their non-sharing, fundamentally dishonest approach, the results they created were the opposite of their intentions.

I do understand why many people do not expose their true feelings with a dying loved one. The fear of death is strong, as is the attachment. However, it is so worth the effort it takes to overcome our own inner holding back that I encourage everyone who has the opportunity to be with a dying friend or relative to take the chance and expose one's true inner feelings. The worst that can happen is a continuation of already existing negativity. The best that can happen (more times than not, it does) is an opening into levels of loving trust and awareness that at the least verifies our living in a highly charged spiritual realm.

Also, it is important to keep our dying loved ones involved in what is happening in the world beyond his or her room. The dying person is the star of an amazingly complex show. And for this show, there is usually no dress rehearsal. Tell them of arrangements you are considering. Discuss wills, funeral arrangements, medical arrangements, everything else. Your loved one may or may not respond. However, as the support person charged with the responsibility for keeping the whole show together, it sure feels good to have the input and reflection from the person for whom you are doing all of this. Therefore, Nancy and I decided early on to keep each other aware of our experiences regarding her dying. For example, we discussed in detail her funeral arrangements. I then did the leg work, made the arrangements and brought the contracts to her, which she read with great interest. The emotional release that occurred while we read through the fine print of a document which described what would happen to her body was intense and refreshing—one less thing for her to think about, one more way to share our love.

Several times I saw her attempting to do something which she was no longer able to do by herself. Sometimes I jumped in and did it for her without consulting her first. Other times I took a less compulsive approach and rather than jump in and do it for her, I shared with her that I would feel better about what she was doing if she would let me help her a little bit. She gladly accepted my offer, knowing that helping her would make me feel good too.

With hindsight I recognize that it would have been better for both of us if I/we had been more communicative as to when help was appropriate and when it wasn't (more on this in the next chapter). As it was, after two years of being prime nurse, chief cook and dishwasher, there were times when I really did not anticipate emptying another bedpan. Generally, though, from our sharing our feelings with each other about each other and our situation, Nancy and I developed a level of closeness that made the whole thing easier for both of us.

HELPING

"Lon, I need help," Nancy would call out.

"Gladly," I'd respond. "What can I do to help?" Frequently my question would be followed by silence. So, I'd go to where Nancy was lying down and try to figure out how she needed help. Sometimes it was obvious, getting something out of reach or emptying the bedpan. Other times I didn't know what help she needed. In that awkward space, I'd be frustrated when my desire to help collided with my not knowing what help was needed. So, I'd putter around by doing something obvious. This situation, my wanting to be of service and then not knowing what was needed when I got there, became one more confusion/difficulty I encountered as Nancy's condition deteriorated. It was only while talking with Jean six months after Nancy died that I was able to gain insight into those times when I was not able to give the help Nancy needed and which she was not able to verbalize.

Jean uses a wheelchair. She has MS. She was explaining to us at a Danica[1] meeting the difficulty she has in getting non-disabled people to see past her disability. "It's as if I don't see me in a wheelchair," she said in her strong, sure voice. "I see myself as getting better and being healthy, that the wheelchair for me is a temporary necessity. But everyone else sees only my wheelchair and doesn't see the healthy person I am inside."

---

1   Danica is an organization in Seattle which provides regular meetings and sharing groups for people with life-threatening and catastrophic illnesses and their support person(s). Nancy got a lot of support from the groups she was involved with. So did I.

"Don't get me wrong," she continued, "I appreciate the changes that have taken place to help: kneeling buses, curb ramps and stair ramps, high tech wheelchairs and other high tech aids. It's much better than a hundred years ago when disabled people were hidden away. You don't see handicapped people in the Old West." (She got me thinking on that one. She's right. With the exception of Chester on "Gunsmoke," I've never seen a handicapped person in a cowboy movie and in any photos of the Old West I've seen in museums.)

"Correct me if I'm wrong," I said, "but your gripe is with non-disabled people who offer help that reinforces the illness rather than meeting the needs of the healthy part of you. For example, seeing you in a wheelchair and opening a door for you (which reinforces your disability *vis-à-vis* my ability) instead of seeing you and saying, 'Hi. How are you doing?' or some other such common conversation starter."

"That's it exactly," Jean responded brightly. "The healthy part of me wants and needs recognition."

Through Jean's help, I saw where I had made mistakes with Nancy. I was seeing Nancy as seriously ill with cancer and physically deteriorating. Consequently, when she asked for help, I responded by providing service in a way which reinforced my seeing her as no longer being able to physically provide for herself. When she couldn't (or wouldn't) tell me what she needed done, I felt frustrated, as did she, and sometimes angry because I had left what I was doing in order to provide for her. I felt like I thought a fireman must feel when he is called out on a false alarm.

What I was not seeing at the time was that when Nancy was asking for help, she was not asking me to do something that would reinforce her inability and thus reinforce the widening physical gap we were feeling. Rather, she was asking me to recognize and connect with that healthy part of her that needed recognition, stimulation and revitalization.

I guess I got so caught up in providing the things she needed to deal with her illness that I forgot to take care of that part of her which was still healthy. We had several arguments which, I now see, were caused by my inability to recognize the difference between the two kinds of calls for help.

The bottom line was that I was providing all the things and encouragement and love that I could for her to get better, which she recognized and appreciated. And I was not recognizing and supporting that part of her which wasn't ill, especially during her last few months when healthy Nancy (the part of her which was still healthy) was crying out, sometimes desperately, to be recognized and supported. I can still hear her in my ears' memory crying, "Help me, please." And me responding, "Here I am. What can I do for you?"

At a Danica meeting, nearly a year after Nancy died, I learned another side of helping, a side I also didn't see while enmeshed in my desire to help Nancy. I learned that it is impossible for one person to provide everything a terminally ill person needs, no matter how much you love them. They need to interact with others in order to deal with everything their illness is stirring up. No one person can be everything for another, especially when the other is dying. What a relief it was for me to hear that. I remembered our arguments, and how I had felt threatened, angry and hurt by Nancy's saying, "I have to go elsewhere to get what I need." She was right. I was attached to doing it all myself, and I was angry with myself for not being able to do/be everything she needed. I'm glad I went to the meeting that night and heard someone else share their experiences and what they learned. Now, I feel better about myself and can forgive myself for what I was not able to do/be for Nancy.

When we speak of loving someone, what we mean is that that person acts as a mirror for the place within us which is love. That being becomes our contact with ourself. When that mirror is shattered, the grief that we feel is the loss of contact with that place within us which is love. Thinking of that person as other than ourself, we mourn our loss, we experience our sense of separateness and isolation that originally motivated us to look outside of ourselves for that essential unity we call love.

STEPHEN LEVINE
WHO DIES?

THE FIRST YEAR

The first year means going through all the birthdays, anniversaries and holidays without your partner, but with the memories. It also means hearing "our" song, visiting or passing "our" favorite places, running into "our" friends, all with their associated memories. The first year can be a year of cleansing, or it can be a year of holding on to the past. It can be the most significant year of my life, or it can be a place to hide. It can be all of these things, or it can be something else entirely.

Here it is, six months later. Nancy's birthday has come and gone. Holidays have come and gone. And for me, they will continue to come and go as long as I'm alive to check off days on a calendar. Once again I'm reminded that things happen. There is no way I can stop them from happening. The only importance something or some event has is that which I give it. Even something which is important to others is not important to me unless I also invest in the idea. For example, Arbor Day didn't mean anything to me until I got to the fourth grade. There, we celebrated the Day (invested ourselves in the consciousness that April 22 was more significant than April 23) by planting a tree.

The importance of Arbor Day has diminished, it seems. It apparently doesn't have the same socio-economic impact as December 25 or July 4. The importance of Arbor Day has so slipped from my consciousness that I had to call the public library to find out when it is. To my surprise, I found that Arbor Day is not a national holiday. Here in the USA, the individual states determine when they will observe it. April is the favored month, with each state having its own formula for determining the exact date. However, International Arbor Day is December

22. I always thought that December 22 was "only 3 more shopping days until Christmas." So much for where we invest levels of importance.

Certain dates were significant in our life only because we made them so. Now that my love/life partner is gone, maintaining significance for specific dates is up to me. I can do it or not do it as I choose. My business sense asks, "What's in it for me?" The answer, of course, is that you get out of it what you put into it.

Remembering: re-membering; putting back together a body of knowledge; reassembling the members in order to recreate a body.

For me, remembering means having to reassemble parts of an experience I've had. In time, some of those parts have deteriorated; others are modified in order to be more acceptable; still others are shifted in importance in order to satisfy current needs. Thus, the event becomes distorted as I attempt to re-member it, and the anniversary date of that event ceases to reflect what actually occurred.

I have chosen to accept each day (including each anniversary) on its own terms, to deal with what comes up on that day as it comes up, to be involved in the events of the day to my fullest ability and to realize that each day is as important/ meaningful as I choose to make it.

Well, my Piscean nature couldn't let that one pass. I reread the above and asked myself, "Lon, aren't you backing off, protecting yourself from possible pain?" No, that's not it at all. For one thing, I'm not backing off. I'm saying that I accept what happens on each anniversary as being what happens. It's my attachment to memories (as distorted as they may be) which invests importance in each day. Should I spend the day crying, as I did on Nancy's birthday, that is exactly what I need to do to get through my grief process. Come our wedding anniversary date, I don't know what I'll feel. But I do know that just because it's our wedding anniversary, I won't make a special effort to wallow around in memories.

Soon after returning to Seattle several months before our wedding anniversary, I went to our favorite restaurant. It's a small place owned by a Vietnamese family. Nancy and I went there on our first date. We continued to eat there often and became good friends with the owners. My first time there alone, I sat at "our" table and had the usual (*cha gio* and curried vegetables with tofu). As I looked at the empty chair beside me, I thought of the last time Nancy and I had eaten there together, and I cried right there in the restaurant.

That whole evening's events, which seemed like only yesterday, replayed themselves in my mind. We had been with friends. Nancy was coughing heavily. I thought she had something caught in her throat. I patted her back to help dislodge the food. That, along with her coughing, caused her tumor to hemorrhage. Our friend, Katherine, who is a nurse, took Nancy to the ladies' room, where they stopped the bleeding and bandaged the tumor. I cleaned up the blood on the chair and floor. Our other friend, Peter, intercepted the curious and took care of the bill. This happened about two months before she died.

Now, many months later, I am back at the restaurant having dinner. It has taken several lunches and dinners to get through the memories, the good and the bad, so that I am able to savor each meal for what it is, instead of investing it with my grief. I choose to continue eating here; I like the people, the food, the prices, the ambiance. It is more important to me to continue this positive relationship than it is to stop coming here because of past associations and memories of past events.

This same holds true for friends of ours. We (the friends and I) know what happened. I'm open to discussing it if they are. I take each relationship for what it is, not for what it was. Consequently, some relationships have stopped, some remain about the same and others have grown to higher and closer levels. Once again, it is all a part of living one day at a time.

FEELINGS—EMOTIONS

We sat sipping sage tea. "It is good for your brain cells," my teacher said, "and for your sore throat. But there is something disturbing you besides your sore throat. Would you like to tell me what it is?"

"Where do I start?" I asked, looking into the reddish-golden liquid in my cup. "It has to do with feelings and emotions. Sometimes I feel like I really have a handle on what's happening with me. I mean, I feel like I really understand what is going on with me and what this grief process is all about. I think things through, and I write things down almost analytically." He looked at me. "Well, all right. I do tend to get analytical. But so what? It helps me keep track of what is going on."

"And?" he asked.

"And," I paused, "there are times when I get completely swamped, overwhelmed with feelings, when my emotions seem to run away with me. I struggle to remember what emotional elimination is and what I can do to continue the process without hurting anyone, including myself. Fortunately, these emotional outbursts are becoming less frequent; yet, I feel like I'm sitting on the rim of Mount St. Helens, like there's this incredible force inside me getting ready to erupt again. I need some help."

"First of all," he began, "you already have a good understanding. Now, however, it is time to take it to the next level, to separate feelings from emotions." He sat back in his chair and took a slow, thoughtful sip of tea. "Our souls, when in their normal, neutral state, buzz along in bliss, joyfully converting God's love energy into loving activity through their vessels, our bodies. However, energies with different frequencies come in and disrupt the bliss frequency, causing the soul to feel differently. Different frequencies of energy flow—vibrations, if you will—cause different feelings. The feelings are received by our finer energy force fields and transmitted to our minds, which interpret the feelings into physical manifestations in our bodies.

"The nervous system, which carries the feelings from the mind to parts in the body, continues the process by carrying messages from the affected parts back to a different part of the mind, which labels and categorizes the feelings and decides what to do with them. Hopefully, mind will let the process continue flowing, letting the feelings flow out of the body as emotions so they are able to dissipate into the ethers.

"Let us say that I am walking along the street and someone approaches. If they are emitting positive intentions toward themselves and others, I will receive their good vibrations in my own energy force field and will have a good feeling regarding them. If they are emitting negative intentions towards themselves and others, my energy force field will receive their bad vibrations. My energy force field acts as a receiving antenna (and sending antenna also) for my soul in the physical world. Otherwise, soul gets energy from God.

"So, this person's vibration enters my force field, causing feelings in me which are sympathetic reflections of the vibrational message being sent. Mind passes on the message to the body parts, which respond accordingly. Responding to the negative intention, my hands sweat, my pulse speeds and my stomach quivers. This activity message goes back to mind, which labels it 'fear,' and my total being begins acting fearful. Curiously, I find my calm inner self 'in fear,' in that it is surrounded by an integrated body/mind which has chosen to manifest fear. I start to run, he chases me. He catches me, takes my wallet, slits my throat and knocks me unconscious. I wake up dead.

"It does not have to end this way. It all depends on how deeply I want to become involved with the emotion. In truth, I can redirect my energy at any step of the way to an expression more likely to yield favorable results. All I need do is remind myself—get it? I re-mind, change the way my mind is working—by saying to myself, 'I am not this fear, this fear is not me. It is passing through and out of me, just as does food, as action and debris.'"

"You're losing me," I said.

"Lon," he said, "our higher self feeds on energy vibrations, just as our lower, physical self feeds on food. This is what Jesus was talking about when he said, 'the bread of God is that which comes down from heaven and gives life to the world.' God's love energy vibration feeds our soul. Thought energy vibrations (our own and others') feed our higher self. Our soul and our higher self are the same. We can keep our soul clean or get it quite dirty, depending on our intentions behind our activities. Ultimately, each one of us determines whether we go to heaven or whether we go to hell."

"You're really losing me now," I said.

"I'm sorry," he said. "I'm losing myself. I got away from the point. Let me try it again. Thought vibrations feed our higher self. We transform thought vibrations within ourselves into feelings, just as we transform food into sustaining nutrients. In either case, we receive input, we digest it, and it becomes our output. Just as 'we are what we eat,' we become what we think. There, that ties it back to the devils and angels. Are you still lost?"

"Not now, thank you." I sipped on my tea.

My teacher continued, "When we put our feelings into action, we emote; we do our emotions. Motion is physical action, emotion is feelings in action.

"Just as we eliminate toxic residue of the food we eat from our bodies through the actions of defecation and urination, so too do we eliminate toxic residue from our thought-energy digestion process through the so-called 'negative' emotions: anger, envy, possessiveness, fear and hatred.

"When we understand that emotions are part of the way in which our body-mind entity keeps itself clean, then we can accept responsibility for eliminating our emotions with discrimination. Just as we do not defecate on our host's carpet, so too do we not throw our anger on the first person who happens by. We use movement (and sometimes vocalizations) to evacuate toxic wastes from our bodies. We can also use movement and vocalization, such as your wood-chopping exercise, to relieve ourselves of toxic emotions. If we hold in emotions or if we hold in our feces and urine, we suffer dis-ease!

"When we see our emotions in such a light, they become less attractive as something to hold on to or to manipulate. It is easier to let them go, to release them, to flush them from our bodies and out into the ethers.

"It is strange to think of ourselves walking around on the bottom of an emotional sewage processing container (can you picture such a thing?), but that is what we are doing. Our planet's etheric atmosphere contains all of our thoughts and all of our emotional eliminations; they are stored in what are called the Akashic Records, those great filing cabinets in the sky.

"In order to survive in this cesspool, we need to eliminate more and more positive emotions, such as happiness and delight, to neutralize the negative ones. We need to continue eliminating our negative emotions also because that will help clear our body-mind so that it can become more in tune with God-Source. For the sake of our environment, though, we need to be more positive in our activities and intentions, starting with viewing our elimination of negative emotions as a positive action.

"You know, the more we laugh, the cleaner the cesspool becomes. Laugh, and the world laughs with you. Our planet, Mother Earth, appreciates kind thoughts toward her too. Treat her gently, and she responds with all we could ever desire. Well, laughter is truly the best medicine. Ask Norman Cousins. He wrote *Anatomy of an Illness*, a fine book.

"Do you need any more help?" he asked, as he poured more tea into our cups.

"No, thank you," I replied. "You've given me more than I know what to do with."

He looked at me and asked, "Does that mean you are unable to comprehend, or does that mean you are skeptical?"

"I am skeptical," I admitted.

"Good," he said, smiling. "Open-minded skepticism is healthy. I admire it. Be skeptical. And the truth is, you have already been applying this knowledge. For proof, just look at yourself. You are moving through the grief process very well."

"Thank you," I said. I was embarrassed.

"You are most welcome, my friend. When you feel stuck and overwhelmed, please remember this: you never get more than you can handle."

DEPRESSION

Depression arrived full tilt this morning. It started with being woken up by a crank phone call and has gone down hill since. I feel worthless, useless, empty. Life is something other people are doing. I do routine activities as if each were a major project. Even a walk outside is something which I have to force myself to do, and once it is under way, I feel as if I'm walking in an envelope, looking through a fogged window, seeing the rest of the world going on about its merry way. Everyone else appears to be very successful, happy to be alive and actively involved in what they are doing. I feel that each step I take is a ponderous movement, as if I am encased in concrete, as if I am not even here.

When I get depressed, I feel especially vulnerable to everything and everyone. Most especially, I feel vulnerable to my own memories. I think of Nancy, and I feel sad. I think of how life was better in the past, and I feel sad. I think about all the mistakes I made in my life, and I feel sad. I think about how if only I had done it that way instead, perhaps everything would be better now, and I feel sad. I look at my life, the stagnation, the frustration, the emptiness, the loneliness, the misery of it all, and my depression goes deeper and deeper.

To say I'm depressed more now that Nancy is dead is not accurate. I go through periods of depression now about as often as I did in the past, before she died. Now, however, the depressions seem deeper, perhaps because of the devastating impact I felt when Nancy died, perhaps because I'm older now and have more missed opportunities to dig up and get depressed about, perhaps both.

I don't know that her death causes my depression. It seems something else will trigger it, and then all the memories feed it. And when things get heavier and deeper, I wish she were here because I desperately need a hug. She isn't here. She's gone— forever. And I need a hug, a gentle reassurance that there is a light at the top of the rut, that this too shall pass. And then I miss her more. I get into my loneliness, and the depression goes deeper.

They say a cure for depression is physical exercise. I don't want to move. They say a cure for depression is being with other people. I want to bury myself under a blanket in the cabin of a drifting sailboat and not come up for three months. They say a cure for depression is Ortho-Phos drops taken in apple cider vinegar and apple juice. I know that one works because Nancy and I have used it before. I'll probably do that one, but not right away. I'm getting some kind of satisfaction from being depressed.

What do I get from being depressed? First, there's the two-sided coin that on one side says only I am depressed; I know that's true because I've been outside and seen other people, and they're all happy and enjoying life. The other side of the coin says I am suffering depression just like everyone else on this planet; therefore I am not alone. Misery loves company. Second, in depression I can feel sorry for myself; I can do and be a "poor me." I can talk with others who suffer depression, and we can commiserate. Third and beyond, I can dump my depression on someone else. I can suck off energy from others as they try to cheer me up. I can be dirty, wear dirty clothes, do dirty work and feed my depression at the same time. I can wallow around in depression as long as I want and not take any responsibility for what is and isn't accomplished. After all, I am depressed. The depression is responsible for what happens to me, not I.

Or is it? I can feel a change happening within me. I am beginning to see my depression and my self as two separate entities. My depression and I are not one. I am not my depression. My depression is not me. My depression is an emotion going through its process, doing its dance. I am not the emotion. I am not the process. I am not the dance. I am the theater in which the dance takes place. I am the audience. Depression is doing this all for me; it's quite a show. I watch, I feel, I laugh with, I cry with. And I am not the depression. The depression is not me. The depression is not responsible for my life. I am responsible for my life. Part of that responsibility is to recognize that depression and all other emotions are transient phenomena which come and go, strutting their stuff on the stage of my mind. It is my responsibility to use my discrimination as to whether or not I want depression, sadness, anger, lust, greed, joy, fear, vanity, happiness or envy to run my life.

To be responsible is to take charge of my life—right now. To shirk my responsibility at this time would be to give in, to let myself be seduced by depression.

This is perhaps the most difficult of the balancing acts we come to learn: to trust the pain as well as the light, to allow the grief to penetrate as it will while keeping open to the perfection of the universe.

STEPHEN LEVINE
WHO DIES?

ABOUT MOURNING

After returning to the Seattle area, I stayed with my cousin until I could find my own residence back in town. She lived in a suburban sprawl house south of the city. Every day she would come home from work and ask me, "Did you find a job yet?"

Every day I would answer, "No."

"Well, why not?" she'd exclaim. "You sit around here all day and do nothing!"

We'd go back and forth, and either she or I would leave the house. And then we'd go through the same thing the next day.

Several times I explained that I was taking care of paper work: insurance forms, social security forms, bank forms and tax forms. (It took almost a month just to straighten out Nancy's and my income taxes from the previous year.) And I told her that I was writing a book about my grief experience. Sometimes she accepted this, sometimes she didn't. I had to remind myself to be gentle with her because she was still hurting from a recent divorce. I also resolved to find my own living space as soon as possible, which I eventually did.

But while I was staying at her house, I came across an ad for a widows' support group. I called about it because I felt the need to be with others who were also going through their private agonies over the deaths of their spouses. The next meeting was scheduled for that evening in a house only a few miles from my cousin's. I went anticipating an evening of sharing and socializing with people who also felt awkward, uncomfortable and on the verge of tears. I was the last to arrive and found nine women and one man chatting.

I felt good. I felt unfettered; I didn't have to explain anything or play any roles because we were all in the same boat. Soon, however, I learned that the women were seeing me as a man first and a widower second. They either wanted to be comforted or they wanted to mother me. No woman really wanted to discuss what grief was about. I went to the other man, and we talked. We shared our losses, we shared our frustrations over not finding the support we really needed, we shared our plans for the future, we shared each other's pain, and we cried together. As we said good night, we shook hands. He was older than I and was uncomfortable when I offered a hug.

I attended two more meetings of this group. The first one was useful; I learned that some of the things I was doing, which I considered bizarre and out of character, were "normal" for a person going through grief. The second meeting was less successful. The group leader had finally returned from her vacation. She seemed nice enough at first, but after awhile, it became clear that she and Big Nurse in *One Flew Over the Cuckoo's Nest* had several things in common.

That night, I was the only man. As we went around the circle and introduced ourselves, the women cried and complained about their feelings of anger, guilt and frustration. The group leader sympathized and offered support for their process. As I introduced myself, I said I did not feel any anger, that I do not believe in guilt, that I believe I was utilized by the Lord to support Nancy's transition and, yes, I did feel grief. The group leader gave me a very harsh look, did not respond and went on to the next person.

As the evening went on, I would raise my hand or offer comments, as did the others. My hand was ignored and my comments were dismissed as irrelevant. I felt like shit. So, I sat there and watched as our group leader played into people's fears and emotions, keeping them caught in their eliminations while slowing creating a dependency relationship which would insure that person coming back to her again and again and again. Needless to say, I did not sign up for her grief-counseling group. I left as soon as the meeting was over, never to return.

I found myself quite alone in my grief. So, I turned to various books to gain insights into how other peoples and other cultures deal with the loss of their members and support the survivors. I learned how they view grief and mourning, and how they care for their own.

From my readings, I've concluded that mourning is the active part of the grief process. It is the sorrow and lamentation we express openly, even publicly, as we go through our grief over the loss of a loved one. The Middle Eastern women and men we see crying over coffins and photographs on the TV news are mourning.

Mourning is a socially acceptable form of emotional release. It is characterized by lasting a specific length of time and by the mourner(s) wearing something conspicuous, usually black clothes or black arm bands, and doing specific activities and/or refraining from doing specific activities. However, different cultures mourn in different ways.

In the Orthodox Hebrew tradition, for example, mourning begins by tearing one's clothes and sitting on a low stool for seven days. Others may visit the mourner, but are encouraged not to carry on unnecessary conversation. Their presence is solace enough. Mourning proceeds in prescribed stages until, at a year less a month, the mourner is fully reintegrated into the social life of the community.

In the Oglala Sioux tradition, the closest surviving (usually male) relative is designated the "keeper" of the departed's soul. For one year, the "keeper of the soul" is excluded from certain activities such as hunting, fighting and using a knife. As for the "kept soul," it is purified through specific rites which allow it and the Spirit to become one so that on the day the soul is released, it will return to the 'place,' *Wakan-Tanka* (God), from whence it came. The kept soul is also viewed as a courier who will take the prayers of the tribe to *Wakan-Tanka* on the day of its release. Thus, the keeper (the mourner) is seen as a holy person whose praying and chanting, which provide emotional release through their intensity and constant doing, is supported by the tribe through gifts of food and other necessities. After the soul is released in an elaborate rite, mourning is over. The tribe celebrates with feasting and rejoicing.

In European cultures, mourners signal to others when they are in mourning by wearing black: the men wear black arm bands and the women wear black dresses and black hats having black veils. If they begin to cry, their behavior is accepted by the others because their black signal has indicated that they are in mourning. A grieving person takes care of him or her self, *vis-à-vis* social interactions, by giving a signal which the society in general recognizes. The society responds by letting them go through their grief without interfering, especially by not asking the question, "What's wrong?"

Although the question is asked with the best intentions, it hinders more than it helps. The mourner, in order to answer the question, has to rearrange his priorities from having an emotional elimination to explaining that nothing is wrong, that everything is actually all right and that they are dealing with the death of a loved one. This answer usually embarrasses the questioner, who then usually says, "I'm sorry," and looks for a way out of the conversation. An appropriate signal read with understanding often prevents such awkward scenes.

My Vietnamese friend pinned a piece of black cloth to her blouse when her father died. For several weeks, I frequently saw her crying while running her very popular restaurant. Because of her cloth signal, practically everyone understood and respected what was happening with her. Her actions showed me that I too could signal to others that my crying was not because something was wrong, but that something was right: I was in mourning and going through my grief.

The signals work. However, it seems that such things are acceptable only on "foreigners," not on "Americans." It seems that outside of ethnic communities our American culture in general does not understand, support and want to accept mourning.

I need an American form of mourning which all Americans recognize and respect. I need to know that when I wear my black arm band, someone won't ask me what I'm protesting against. I need to know that when I start weeping on the bus, the other riders will at least be caring enough to not look at me like I'm crazy. I need to know that not just the Hispanics and Italians and Central Europeans and Northern Europeans and other so-called "foreigners" understand mourning, but also the third-generation children of these "foreigners." I need to know that it is safe for me, a man, to mourn openly.

I'm tired and confused. I'm confused by our transient, short-sighted society. I'm confused by a national mythology which deifies the fanatical, repressive Puritans, while destroying respect for all living things as practiced by the American Indians. I'm confused by my German-Austrian heritage which denies itself, in the wake of two world wars, in order to appear more American. I'm confused by why we continue to define ourselves by how much we withhold, instead of by how much we give. I feel like I'm on the outside looking in, a man expressing his sorrow and feelings of loss, looking in at a society in which men don't cry unless they are "foreigners," crazy or gay.

I'm tired of it all. I'm tired of denying what I am—a straight, heterosexual man with feelings, deep feelings, and lots of them. It's enough to make one frustrated and angry, which, of course, is what it does. And the price we men pay for going along with this twisted view of how things should be is heart attacks, stressed out hearts giving up under the burden of carrying so much emotional crap inside.

We men, for our own preservation, need to honor and accept our feelings. We men need to support each other as we express our feelings, not just joy, with a shared "high five," but also pain and grief with, if not a shoulder to cry on, at least a caring touch. If we don't do this for each other, brothers, who will?

When will we stop hiding behind our fears? When will we stop using our minds for creating thoughts and things which deny our interdependence? When will we accept that we are created in God's image, not He in ours? When will we accept our humanity? We are all living beings, fragile living beings, dependent on an equally fragile planet to sustain our being alive. We all enter the world through the womb. We all die. We all know others who have died. And our hearts ache from carrying the tears we are afraid to let flow.

Sometimes I think that we as a nation suffer from uncompleted grief, holding inside the pain that has plagued us for at least 25 years. Beginning with the assassinations of John and Robert Kennedy and Martin Luther King, Jr., building with the destruction of our sense of national pride in Vietnam and our disappointment with Richard Nixon, and continuing to today's declining economy, our scattered political presence and our shattered confidence in the credibility of the people who maintain our systems, we have a lot to mourn over and a lot of grieving to finish. Otherwise, we will forever wallow in our own inertia, while continuing to stifle the needed emotional elimination which would set us free to build a nation that feels good to be in again. Is it no wonder that we are riddled with cancer, the disease many believe has its roots in emotional stagnation?

For starters, perhaps we as a nation would do well to have one big cry over our losses in Vietnam and then be done with it, instead of continuing to let it fester until it becomes ill-aimed anger reactions such as "Rambo" and our recurring MIA obsession.

We have cried together before: on November 11—Veteran's Day—when the Tomb of the Unknown Soldier reminds us of the waste created by war, and on November 22, 1963, the day President Kennedy was killed.

Perhaps we Americans are now in the process of defining our own form of mourning. People weep openly at Vietnam memorials across our land. Athletes, both professional and scholastic, are being more open in their personal sorrow over a loss. Television news shows the tears and anguish of people (farmers, workers, students, husbands, wives, children, lovers) dealing with the loss of relatives, friends and livelihoods. The *Challenger* disaster put death in our living rooms, giving us the opportunity to share the grief of those New Hampshire school children and of our President.

But before we have a national "Day of Mourning" or an American style of mourning, we need to individually accept mourning as something we will do when the situation calls for it. Each of us mourns in our own way. However, to not allow oneself to mourn is to deprive oneself of one of life's most profound self-openings. Are you ready?

In our lifetime, we have many opportunities/challenges which allow us to experience our emotional selves at levels on which we do not usually operate. Marriage, the birth of a child, attainment of a personal goal and major rejection (e.g., being fired) all expand our emotional selves and our awareness of our emotional selves. It often feels that these and similar events take us to our self-perceived limits of our emotional selves. But these experiences pale in comparison to the emotional extremes we can reach while going through and eliminating our grief over the loss of a loved one.

For myself, I experienced every emotion I had ever experienced before: sadness, joy, uncertainty, fear, relief, confusion, "the fog" (when I feel that everything I'm doing is being done and perceived as if I were in a thick fog), "cotton-headed" (withdrawing inside my head so far that there seems to be an insulating layer of cotton between me and the inside of my skull, which makes interacting with the rest of the world a painfully slow process), nastiness, hypersensitivity, insensitivity, composure, agony, love, hate, anxiety and inner peace—at levels more intense than at any time previously. *Plus*, new emotions appeared and made their debut expression through me.

For example, I felt compassion for *all* living beings for the first time. I'd felt sympathy and empathy before, but never total compassion. It was a euphoric feeling, similar to the bliss I felt while driving down the freeway after giving an elderly man CPR. It was the first time in my life I had been with someone at their moment of death. I heard the death rattle in his breath just as Medic One arrived. I left the scene feeling empty and blissful and very aware of how tenuous our hold on life really is. As I drove down the freeway, I noticed the people driving their cars instead of noticing the cars. I was aware of people's faces as they drove: happy faces, worried faces, anxious faces and calm faces. And I was aware of each driver having his or her own life with its own set of circumstances. I experienced total, unqualified acceptance of everything and everyone being exactly as they ought to be, that all that is, is perfect. (I learned later the elderly gentleman had recovered; I was credited with saving his life. Will wonders never cease?)

In that moment of bliss on the freeway and in that euphoric feeling of compassion for all living beings I felt after Nancy died, I must have experienced what others have described as feeling at one with the universe, as going with the flow. At those times, I felt an incredible clarity in my perceptions and an ease of expression which allowed me to do whatever I needed to be doing while also feeling that whatever I was doing was absolutely right with the general flow of everything. I felt wonderful. I'd like to do it again!

Looking back on my mourning, I recognize two keys which helped me unlock myself: first, to allow myself to feel and express in a socially responsible way whatever emotions came up and second, to not be afraid of the power and/or intensity of those emotions. What helped me to do the second part was to remind myself that the emotion and the power behind the emotion are not the same thing. My power is there in me all the time, "powering" all aspects of my being. When my anger and other emotions come up and out especially strongly or powerfully, it is not the emotion which is powerful, rather, it is my own general-purpose power applied to the emotion which makes the emotion appear so strong. I can apply the same amount of power to any of my emotions, just as I can apply the same amount of power to any of my other activities. This thought helped me get past the idea that one emotion is more powerful than another.

Perhaps you know someone who is afraid of their own anger because it comes out so powerfully. They tend to view their anger as potentially dangerous to themselves and others. They often say something like, "I don't like to get angry because when I do, I'm afraid I'll hurt somebody." So, instead of releasing their anger in responsible little bits, they hold it inside where it builds and builds until there is an explosion. How often do we see in the news the "nice, quiet guy" who, one day, pulls out a gun and kills his workmates and himself.

By remembering that all emotions get their power from the same source and by separating power from manifestations, we can accept any emotion without being afraid of it. And we know that when an emotion manifests very powerfully, we can redirect the bulk of the power to other aspects of our being without taking away from the emotion or stopping it from leaving. The emotion will still be eliminated (as long as we don't shut it down), yet it won't make such a fuss during its departure.

For example, anger power can be redirected to manifest as enthusiasm, while the anger itself evaporates like steam into the atmosphere. Depression power can be redirected into exercise, and the depression will still be eliminated like steam into the atmosphere. I eliminated lots of anger with Broom Therapy, in which I swept sidewalks, walls, floors, everything. (I've developed a strong dislike for those motor-powered blowers. They not only are noisy, polluting, and petroleum consumers, they also vibrate your body, hurt your ears and deprive you of the benefits of a healthy, relaxing exercise. Besides that, they don't even clean. They merely redistribute the dirt or leaves. Give me the soothing swish-swish of a broom or leaf rake any day. I also prefer my old hand-pushed lawn mower for the same reasons.) Keith, a fellow widower, kept telling me, "The only thing that keeps me from going bonkers from grief is my 45-minute walk every day. Some days I walk longer. Exercise is the key. It gets the endorphine gland [sic] going so you have energy to beat hell. And you feel good."

Keith's comments on exercise point back to the first key: to express emotions in a socially responsible way. Here the challenge is to be responsible and to have our emotional eliminations in ways which harm neither ourselves nor others. A trick which helps do this is to be the nonattached observer watching the process happen without getting trapped in it. By watching how thoughts, events and emotions unfolded, I could use my discrimination to choose a way for eliminating emotions which would not dump on others and was constructive, not destructive.

When some guy ran into my car with his car, we yelled and huffed and puffed and exchanged insurance numbers. For the rest of the day, I was angry with him. But he was hours from me and miles from my neighborhood. Still, I was angry with him. So, instead of taking my anger out on the next person to phone me while I was doing something I did not want interrupted, I chopped wood for my fireplace. I redirected my anger power into chopping wood, all the while imagining that guy's head on the chopping block. I ended the day with my anger released—which helped me be clear in my dealings with the insurance company the next day—and a nice pile of firewood.

My teacher says emotional release is one of the natural eliminative processes our living body-mind uses to cleanse itself. Otherwise, old feelings and emotions held inside fester and rot like garbage, causing both physical and spiritual dis-ease. Now I know why I feel good after going to a baseball game: I get to yell at the umpire, boo the other team and jump up and down for the home team. What a release!

For those of you suffering the anguish of major loss, please do not hold back. Let your grief flow. Let your emotions eliminate through their expression. Cry if you want to, and cry some more. It's okay. It really is. Mourning the death of a loved one is a rare and precious opportunity. As more of us acknowledge the healing we receive from going through the grief process and more of us discover the positivity inherent in grieving, we will affect changes, and our society will become more supportive of men in mourning.

BIZARRE BEHAVIOR

As the shock of Phase I lifted, I got into going through (and recognizing my going through) the erratic behavior of Phase II. Fortunately, I had the sensible advice of my friend, Rev. Randy Laakko, buzzing around in my brain. He said, "Don't be surprised by anything that happens. For people in grief, anything can happen. You'll do things you least expect. It's okay."

There were several bits of what is, for me, abnormal behavior; some I did, some I considered. For example, I considered becoming a gun runner to the rebels in Central America. It seemed perfectly reasonable because at that point I didn't give a hoot about anything anyway. After serious consideration, I dropped the idea.

I did some things which, at the moment of their doing, seemed totally appropriate, yet after their doing were immediately discarded. Flashes in the pan. For example, I felt a compulsion to put on Nancy's favorite dress. It didn't fit. I split the seams. But for a moment, I felt she was with me again. I could feel her presence, smell her scent, see movement in that piece of cloth again. Then I thought about how silly I must look and felt embarrassed and confused by what I had done. So, I took it off, packed it away, and that was that. Later, at a meeting of widows and widowers, I learned that it is not uncommon for women to wear shirts and pants of their husbands. They get a sense of comfort from the feel of the clothes, a sense of their dead husbands' presence. I was too embarrassed to say what I had done. Yet, I'm saying it now because I can't help but feel that out there somewhere is a brother going through his grief over the death of his wife and, as a part of his grief, has put on some of his wife's clothes and is embarrassed and confused by his action. Well, brother, don't take it seriously. Get a laugh from it. It's all part of the grief process "crazies."

In retrospect, I see those "crazy" actions and thoughts as having fulfilled some sometimes unexplainable needs of my grief process. For example, walking on hot, burning coals in my bare feet was one of my "crazy" activities. Yet from it, I learned about fear and how to change fear from an obstacle to an ally.

Randy's advice to not be surprised by anything that happens, that I'll do things I least expect and that it's okay, has been very helpful. By keeping it in mind, I have been able to move through my thoughts and activities without getting caught up in what I was doing. I know that without his advice, I could have easily become ensnared in each incident and would have spent unknown quantities of time and energy dissecting the "whys and wherefores" of everything that happened. All of that dissecting would have gotten me attached to my eliminations because of the time and energy invested in examining them. This would not only have slowed the flow of my grief process considerably, it would also have turned the whole process into one of interminable sadness and negativity.

I consider myself fortunate to have had the preparation and support I've had. It has made my grief process lighter, friendlier and generally very positive. Everything is flowing along exactly as it ought to. Thoughts come up, thoughts fly away. Some are acted upon, some are discarded. And some are written down for reflection and/or sharing.

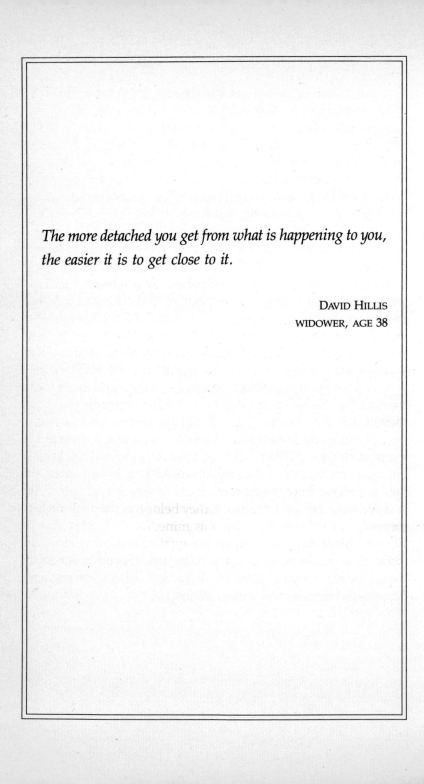

The more detached you get from what is happening to you, the easier it is to get close to it.

DAVID HILLIS
WIDOWER, AGE 38

OBSERVING WITHOUT GETTING CAUGHT UP IN WHAT YOU SEE

My brother and I were talking; he had just finished reading an early draft of all this writing. He said, "You say several times that I should observe but not get caught up or trapped in whatever it is I'm feeling or whatever is going on with my life. But you don't tell me how to. I need some 'how tos' on watching my feelings without being dragged along by them. That's what you mean by not getting caught up in them, isn't it?"

"That's right, Bro," I answered. I told him that I have a technique which allows me to watch my thoughts and feelings as they play out before me like a movie on a screen in my head. It's as if I'm watching my mind in a mirror, watching the show it puts on.

I quoted Dr. Randolph Stone, who said, "I am not these: Grief, Desire, Anger, Attachment or Fear. I am the Seer. I am seeing them. They are not mine, they belong to the various Elements. I should not claim these as mine."

I told him that by practicing mental detachment, I could "see" how my activities and reactions really aren't me, but rather reactions, like conditioned responses, which the functional mind uses. It's as if the way in which my physical and mental self functions is like a computer performing programs. My inner self (my seer, true self, soul essence) is the computer operator watching the process and giving commands which the computer will, hopefully, follow and not reject, because it (the computer) thinks it has a mind of its own. Then I explained the technique I use which allows me to separate and watch my thought processes.

I use a basic meditation exercise which goes like this:

1. Sit in a comfortable position which allows you to sit still.

2. Minimize distractions. Unplug the phone, turn things off, eliminate or mask stimulating odors (such as cooking food).

3. Tune out/don't pay any attention to distractions.

4. Notice how you stopped paying attention to distractions.

5. Notice yourself noticing how you stopped paying attention to distractions.

6. Staying at this same level of consciousness in which you notice that you notice, notice how your mind creates its own distractions and how your mind tries to pull "you" into them.

7. Notice how you get pulled into a mind movie and what that does to you physically and emotionally.

8. Try it again.

Another technique for practicing observing without getting caught in what you see is known as "contemplative prayer." The Christian minister from whom I learned this technique explained that she used contemplative prayer to understand who she was and what she needed to be doing. It was her way to get to the heart of a matter. As Rev. Martin said, "I use contemplative prayer to get honest about myself and my dealings. Honesty clarifies; dishonesty muddles."

Her approach to contemplative prayer has two parts.

Part 1: Clear the thought-space inside by doing a specific set of mental exercises. (She explained her clearing process. It was much the same as my previously mentioned meditation exercise.)

Part 2: Listen! allowing God's voice to come through.

"Well, that helps," my brother said. "I don't know if I can do it exactly as you say, but I'll give it a try. By the way, could you send me something that would help me understand this whole thing better?"

"Sure," I said.

We ended our long distance conversation, and I turned to my library, hoping to find a book with the right words that would help make things clear. I found what I was looking for in the marvelous book *Im Kopf—In the Head*. This book was created and illustrated by the gifted London artist, Peter Schmidt, who also created the Ten Freedoms found in Appendix I of this book. *Im Kopf—In the Head* is a picture book. There are very few words, as words could not describe all the opportunities for self-reflection the artist presents. I've taken his core drawing and have added embellishments and captions in order to make my point. Since a picture is worth a thousand words, perhaps these pictures will help explain the process well enough for a person to see how his or her mind works and how he or she could create their own "how to" program of actions, activities and thought processes which would enable them to detach themselves from the activities of their mind.

This is the me the world sees and interacts with.

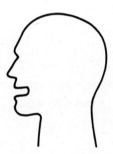

Inside the me the world sees is another me.

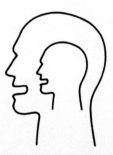

When everything is going smoothly, communication is straight, and I'm responding to the world/to other people clearly and harmoniously, and I feel good about it all, I look like this.

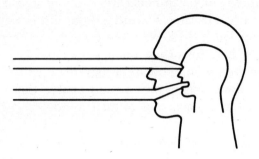

When I'm feeling out-of-it, out of step with the world, and responding perfunctorily without care or interest, I look like this.

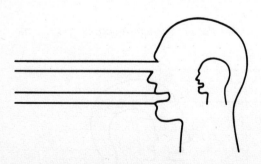

When I'm aware of what is going on, but not able
to share how I feel about it,
I'm like this.

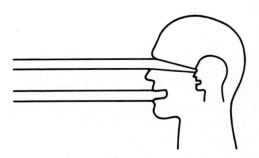

When I'm not aware of what is going on with others
and seem to interrupt their lives with my own tunnel
vision that hits them like a bolt out of the blue,
so that I come off as insensitive to their needs
(and consequently can't understand why
they are treating me so callously),
I'm like this.

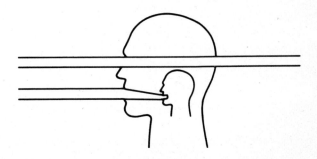

And when I'm caught up in my own inner self
(emotions, etc.), so that I begin acting out my
perceptions of myself even when those perceptions
have absolutely nothing to do with what is really
going on around me,
I'm like this.

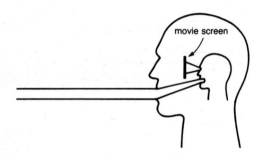

When I feel quite alone, but don't know why,
I remind myself that within me is also my Seer,

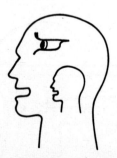

who reminds me to do this
(turn off the mind movie
and see what's beyond the screen),

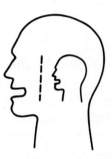

so that I can get back to this.

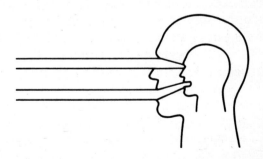

HOW LONG
DOES GRIEF LAST?

The other day I was talking with Skip, who shared with me some of his favorite passages from a book called *Creative Divorce* by Mel Krantzler. Skip's wife had recently divorced him. In talking with him, it became clear to me that there are definite similarities between the grief one feels on losing a spouse through divorce and losing a spouse to death. In many ways the grief process is the same. The differences, of course, are that in death the spouse is physically out of your life, and you have no say in the situation, whereas in divorce your "ex" is still around (maybe annoyingly so), and you have some level of control over the situation.

But what intrigued me the most in our conversation was a statistic and a list of indicators. The statistic is the average period of time needed to get through the grieving process, 1.8 years. Now applying that to my own situation, I don't know if that means I'll put in a total of 1.8 years crying, or if after 1.8 years everything will begin getting better or what. To me, statistics have been a way of translating human functions into mathematics. Since human functions vary so considerably, the statistics don't mean a whole lot. However, they do give a ballpark figure. For example, if I'm a ball player, it would help me to know if I'll be playing my next game in Philadelphia or Los Angeles. So, that 1.8 figure tells me I won't be doing this forever, and that in about two years, things will settle down considerably. Please don't worry if it's taking you longer; we all move at our own pace.

The list of indicators, modified to fit a surviving spouse's needs, is as follows.

Grieving is over:

> when resentment and longing cease to be obsessions, but become occasional flashes;
>
> when less time is spent complaining about problems and more time is spent solving problems;
>
> when I begin re-establishing old friendships, establishing new friendships and creating new relationships;
>
> when decisions are based on my interests and on what pleases me;
>
> when I no longer feel the need to feel guilt or to place blame;
>
> when I realize that the loss is not a failure on my part or on anyone else's;
>
> when I let go of the "if onlys";
>
> when I accept that I'm not the only person to have this happen to me;
>
> when I can see beyond the events in my life and can cease defining myself by them;
>
> when I can observe my attachments and release them, without getting caught up in them again;
>
> when I feel optimistic, back to life and can make it on my own.

Your grief is your own.
It does not come from someone else.

REV. RANDALL LAAKKO
(FROM A CONVERSATION WE HAD WHILE SITTING IN HIS VOLVO,
MARCH 1984)

THE FIRST ANNIVERSARY

Tonight there is a full moon. Full moons have always been special for me. Nancy and I were married on the night of the full moon. Each full moon was our anniversary. We counted our time together in full moons. We often joked about the time we would be saying, "Many moons ago, we . . ."

One year ago yesterday, I saw her alive for the last time. One year ago yesterday, we embraced for the last time. One year ago yesterday, we shared our special thoughts and feelings for each other for the last time. In a little less than two weeks from today, it will be one year since I received the phone call that told me of her death. In two weeks from today, to the day, it will be one year since I saw Nancy's body in the funeral home in Mexico. It was a year ago that Nancy and I shared our last full moon together in San Diego.

There is something special about the first anniversary. During this time, you may remember or even relive in your mind all those events, all those feelings of one year ago. Events that happened a year ago are still relatively fresh in the mind, especially big events like this one. Three hundred and sixty-five days seems to be just the right amount of time to have gone and done a full Earth's cycle worth of activities, without losing a grasp on an event which happened "only a year ago." After passing the one year mark, the specifics of the event begin to fade as new memories of the current season's events come in. Environment, weather, seasons of the year, cultural activities become the cues and signals we use to play back memories and program in new ones. We do this automatically. That great sponge in our skull that we call our brain loves to collect and store perceptions (memories) to be used or misused as we so desire.

As I am going through the first anniversary of Nancy's transition, I'm barraged by reminders of the events of last year. Some reminders are intentional, like looking at my diary for 1983. Some are unintentional, like the cold, rainy Seattle weather, the same that greeted me as I stepped off the plane from warm, sunny San Diego last year. These reminders (especially for me, the weather and my sensitivity to the approaching holidays) almost make the first anniversary feel like an obstacle, an event unto itself. It's an obstacle in the sense that once I'm over it, I've passed a notable major milestone *vis-à-vis* my transition from the shock and deep grief that accompanies still being very close to the event, to the intermittent grief and the feeling of beginning to break out of my cocoon which accompanies the distancing from the event. The old saying, "Time heals all wounds," is totally appropriate and ever more meaningful.

Once the first anniversary is passed, the event that gave November 20 its anniversary status is literally something that happened a year ago. I am no longer living in that year, in that 365-day cycle, in which the event took place. The first anniversary also indicates that time has passed—as always, sometimes too quickly, sometimes too slowly. And yes, I do feel better than I did a year ago. So, in a sense, I am proving the truth of the saying, "Time heals all wounds."

It may be that I'm making too much of this one year thing. However, I think not. After all, each of us celebrates annual events in our lives, from birthdays to cultural holidays, all determined by the return of the planet Earth to a fixed spot in space in relation to the sun. To make it easier for us to determine which of the Earth's daily advancements in its orbit is the appropriate one for celebrating the annual event, we use calendars, be they pinup, digital, Mayan, or Stonehenge. That's the way we humans have been doing it for years.

And so, another full moon passes, stirring up the memories of events a year ago. With the memories comes internal agitation. With the internal agitation come feelings of sadness and vulnerability. With those feelings come tears. These days have not been easy. Yet, in each day enough change takes place to keep me putting one foot in front of the other as I continue moving through this great gift called life.

The idea that crises have negative and positive aspects is captured in a word the Chinese have for crisis, wei-chi. The first part of the word means "beware, danger." The second part, however, has a very different implication; it means "opportunity for change."

PETER RUSSELL
THE GLOBAL BRAIN

CHRISTMAS 1984

Last Christmas I was in shock. Nancy was dead four, maybe five weeks. I had just finished selling, packing and moving things out of our apartment, which I had to vacate by December 15. And I was 3,000 miles east with my family in Delaware. I was in shock. Christmas came and went—for me, a nonevent filled with ritual and emptiness.

This year is different. I am definitely not in shock. I'm settled into my new apartment, a comfortable one-bedroom with a fireplace, and I'm very much aware of what is going on both inside and outside of me. Inside, I'm feeling a sense of deep relief from having gone through this whole thing and surviving it as well as I have. I feel I can breathe again without having to remind myself to. And I feel deep gratitude to all my friends and relatives who were there when I needed them.

Outside, the media extols the "-nesses": happiness, family-ness, togetherness. People are busy buying, running hither and thither, preparing—a hustle-bustle that fills the air with electricity and excitement. A street corner Santa plays saxophone, hoping to catch stray coins in his kettle. On another corner, three girls tap-dance to this year's version of yester-years' hits. Children sit on the "real" Santa's knee in the department store window, while tired parents take a breather. It feels good being downtown, moving in that warming buzz that accompanies people caught up in a common, happy purpose.

Yet, little things creep in, innocent in themselves until I give them another meaning. A lady asks me to hold out my hand to help her judge which gloves would fit her husband best. This year, I'm buying my own gloves. Lovely frillies entice me as I walk through the store wishing I had someone to give them to. Excited children pick out things for Dad. I wish they were the children that I had thought about having. I feel suddenly old, remembering my childhood. I go home.

My token Christmas decoration greets me, an evergreen spray on the door, the only decoration on my side of the building. Inside, TV shows me what I don't have. I remind myself to buck up, be thankful for what I have and be thankful that I'm still here. After a good cry, I remind myself that it's not time to leave this planet just yet because I haven't finished my book.

This is the holiday season, the holy day season. The holy days are what this period of time is all about. However, as much as I work at reminding myself about this, I feel a lot of grief. I stagger through each day, keeping busy just to keep busy. Last week, I rode a horse for the first time. Two weeks before, I walked on fire. A month before that, I rode in a hot air balloon. Of the three, I prefer riding horses, which I'll do again on the 24th. And in between, I go to the movies. Yesterday, it was *Dune*. Today it is *Amadeus*. Mozart's industry made such an impression on me that I started writing again. Writing also serves to give my life some meaning right now, in addition to keeping me busy. And when the activity stops, it's me again, feeling absolutely lonely. The challenge is in maintaining balance.

I want to love, to share with, to give to; and it's hard, because the one I love is no longer here. As a way of consolation, I tell myself that I'm not alone. I think of people everywhere who have lost family—in India, in Ethiopia, across the street. But that doesn't lessen my inner pain. I'm feeling miserable and I know it. To deny my sadness, to deny my grief would be to invalidate the reality of my feelings. Instead, I can feel compassion ("co-passion") with the man in India or the woman in Ethiopia. I do not diminish my own grief out of sympathy for their suffering. Rather, I gain strength from knowing that we are united in our common bond of grief. (Writing *that* gives me goose bumps.) Our grief unites us. It's a special bond available to all. It is most significantly shared by those who open themselves to it unselfishly, unceremoniously, whole-heartedly.

To recognize the universality of grief and sorrow is to also recognize the universality of love. And isn't love what Christmas is all about?

1985

The pain of leaving those you grow to love is only the prelude to an understanding of yourself and others.

SHIRLEY MACLAINE
"DON'T FALL OFF THE MOUNTAIN"

ATTACHMENT

When I was a Cub Scout, I built a balsa wood model race car. I painted it black with red seats, and bent wires for the grill and windshield frame. After a few years, I outgrew it. It was primitive compared to the models I was then making. My younger brother wanted it, but I didn't want him to have *my* car, so I destroyed it. I was really attached to it being my car, and I didn't want anyone else, especially my little brother, to have it and enjoy it.

I recall now that during my childhood and adolescence, people considered me greedy. I kept to myself and didn't share much of either my things or my interests. As I grew older, I learned to share (share living space, share resources, share myself) by opening up, taking a chance, slowly putting myself out there with others, eventually even letting someone borrow my real car. That was a major "letting go" for me. After all, it was *my* car.

As I opened to others, others opened to me. Relationships developed. Some burst full bloom, then withered the next day. Others took days, weeks, years to develop. One relationship was still going strong ten years later when she said, "I don't want to see you again. Good-bye." At that moment of truth, I realized that I had changed over the past couple of years, and she hadn't. If I wanted to keep our relationship going, I would have to change back to where she and I could relate once again. I liked my new me. I still do, So, I said good-bye, and that was that. A relationship that I had been attached to for ten years was suddenly, completely over. I gave up my attachment to her and to our relationship (not without some tears over the loss of this comfortable situation), eliminated that relationship from my life and started over—the power of a clean good-bye. As it turned out, this opened the door to my heart once again, and in walked Nancy.

She and I married and established ourselves in Seattle. We managed an apartment building to help make ends meet. After two years, we were terminated and given two weeks to leave. This meant finding another place to live, another job, and moving—all in two weeks. This hurt us both, as we were also coming to the realization that Nancy's cancer was serious and needed special care.

We struggled through giving up our attachments to being where we were (in our first home) and taking just anything. Instead, we focused our attention on getting exactly what we needed. Even though this was difficult for us and kept us on a nervous edge, we felt we had to. We felt we had to accept the challenge of the moment and use it to grow to something better. We did not want to feel sorry for ourselves and take something that was convenient but less than we needed, which would have ultimately caused us to wither. For a reminder to ourselves to not get caught up in the drama of our situation, we put up a picture of a chubby, buddha-like man who was laughing uproariously. If you are familiar with Ram Dass, you may know this picture; it's of his spiritual master, Neem Karoli Baba. Whenever we felt we were drowning in our own tears, we looked at his picture and laughed. By the end of the month, we had accepted an offer to manage a prestigious apartment building which provided us with exactly what we needed. The building was called The Ramayana, after the title of the ancient Indian epic which tells the story of Ram and his lessons in overcoming attachments. There are no accidents in this universe.

We didn't know it at the time, but this business of dealing with our desire to stay in our first home gave us an opportunity to learn how to let go of attachments and to go with the flow of the process of change. It was a rehearsal for what happened later.

When it became clear that Nancy was about to die, we shared that our greatest attachment was to each other. We overcame it (slowly, reluctantly and with lots of tears) by accepting the flow of events and by recognizing that our mutual attachment, our inner and outer clinging to each other, was a distraction which would keep her increasing spiritual energy from focusing itself for her impending journey out of her body. We said our good-byes. At a time when all was right, she made her transition unimpaired.

Nancy's request was that her physical remains, her ashes, be placed at the Karma Triyana Dharmachakra (the KTD, as it is commonly called), a Tibetan Buddhist spiritual center in upstate New York. I did so. For months after, I felt that I wanted to live within driving distance of the KTD so that I could visit her often. I thought that I would be able to maintain a relationship with her every time I visited the site. I wanted to believe she resided at the KTD, that she lived there, so to speak.

What had prompted me to consider moving close to the KTD was my attachment to Nancy's physical presence. But this would be a strictly one-sided relationship based on my attachment, my longing to still have her with me. I can only imagine that my feeling was not unlike the comfort others may find in knowing that their loved ones are in the local cemetery. However, maintaining my attachment to Nancy's physical remains was not done to do her service. Rather, it was done to give me a way to deal with my reluctance to accept that she is really dead and no longer a part of my life.

I returned to the KTD on her birthday, three months after placing her remains with the abbot. I put flowers on the altar in her memory, prayed a lot and took a walk in the surrounding forest. During the drive back to New York City, I realized that I no longer needed to visit the KTD to be with her. She wasn't really there. Her spirit/soul is with God. Only her ashes remain in upstate New York, and they are rapidly decomposing and becoming one with the Earth.

As I travel further from the event of her death, I recognize that my attachments to her are nothing more than memories which I alone carry around. For example, a chance hearing of a song that we had enjoyed together starts me crying, only because I have given that song my own particular meaning. The same song does other things for other people. We all have our own attachments.

Attachment is perhaps the dominant theme in human affairs. Attachment starts as an emptiness inside, a desire for someone or something to come into our lives and make us complete. We say, "If I only had ＿＿, then ＿＿." Next comes the search for ＿＿. The search consumes a surprisingly large amount of energy, time and effort. The search puts us to work, helps us choose the people we want to associate with and activates our desires for more and more, bigger and better. The search is the psychological underpinnings of consumerism, materialism and religionism.

As a consequence of the search, we find. That which we search for (or in some cases, the image of that which we search for) attracts us to it, and we find it. After we find the object of our search, our desire emotionally bonds us to that object. The object can also be and often is another person. As the bonding strengthens, the bond, like well-cured glue, becomes attachment. We become emotionally, psychologically and physically bonded to the object of our desires, and over a period of time, to the experiences the objects provide for us. We even structure our lives in order to meet the demands of our attachments. Then, we settle into our new pattern and hope we now have it all. Thus, attachment becomes the sum total of our mental, emotional, psychological and physical experiences regarding the recognition of, the need for, the search for, the attainment of and the experience of an object/person of our desires.

Attachment is also wanting things to not change. Attachment is wanting things, events, people and situations to remain the same. Our attachment to a person or situation grows from the comfort of familiarity. Familiarity is predictable. What is familiar and predictable is safe. For us to be safe emotionally, physically, psychologically and spiritually, we desire no change. Eventually, we become so attached to the thing, person, situation, or belief that we spend our lives protecting our investment, as it were, instead of changing to something that is often better for us. The challenge is to overcome our attachment, our clinging, to that which appears safe for us, but which is often not safe at all, merely undemanding. Accepting change as a positive good stimulates us and allows us to grow.

Like the baby who cries out when he is pulled away from the breast, we too react to changes in comfortable situations and relationships. The extent to which we react is often based on fear, the fear that that which is safe, comfortable, undemanding and unchallenging will not return again. Once a person's attachment has been turned from enjoyment of "it" (whatever "it" is) to fear of losing "it," then that person holds the potential for becoming an active neurotic and a socially disruptive unit. It seems that a great many people function at the level of fear of the possibility of losing that which they have become attached to, even though this often means going against the flow of change in order to reinstate and replicate a relationship or situation which was good for them at one time, but which may no longer be valid.

As long as attachment is kept in its dark side, fear, there will be military establishments with offensive overkill capabilities and judiciary, legislative and police establishments which suppress many, many facets of the human experience.

Fear affects personal relationships too. They deteriorate into play-acting, in which the participants play safe, predictable roles with each other, even though the roles do not reflect the current realities and needs of the persons playing them. Through playing roles with each other, we satisfy needs we needed filling at one time, but which for us now may be nothing more than crumbs. The unfortunate aspect of this is that so many people are willing to accept crumbs from life, instead of letting go of their attachments.

When attachment basks in its light side, fulfillment and enjoyment, there is sharing, caring and daring: sharing, so that others too may enjoy; caring, so that others too will be fulfilled; and daring, to express the Divine within us all. By accepting that God's love is with-in and with-out as a simultaneous, never-ending event, it becomes easier to take the next step with attachment, which is to lovingly and voluntarily give it up.

Many spiritual master-teachers have shown us by their examples that it is possible to give up our desires for material things, for sensually inspired relationships and for intellectual masturbation. And they have demonstrated time and again that the more you give up, the more you get back. Jesus gave the supreme example by allowing himself to be crucified. He gave up his physical body and received Eternal Life, infinite existence which transcends the limitations of the human form. Admittedly, Jesus' example is more than most of us are willing to follow. In fact, it is difficult for me to give a cold stranger my coat, even when I know I have two more coats hanging in the closet. Attachment lies deep. It is no lightly bubbling stream running on the surface of the human psyche. Rather, it is a deep coursing river, unseen, crisscrossing the inner depths of the human experience. It is not easy to give up attachments to our things and to our loved ones.

Fortunately, however, life gives us many opportunities to practice (learn by doing) giving up attachments. My personal favorite is the garage sale. I never cease to be amazed by how good I feel after ridding myself of what were such indispensable parts of my life (and are now indispensable parts of someone else's life) as I have at my garage sales. Some day soon, I'd like to have a spiritual garage sale where I can rid myself of outmoded and superfluous concepts.

Another opportunity to practice giving up attachments is by donating to charitable organizations. I'm not referring to getting the Salvation Army to haul away a broken refrigerator and leaving you a tax deduction in its place. I'm referring to giving extra clothing we could still wear but don't, or giving serviceable household items we could still use but don't want to, and giving these either through a charitable organization or directly to a fellow human being we see needing.

A third way to learn what it feels like to release attachment to our material world and to replace that attachment with an appreciation for our world and what it offers is to tithe. Ten percent. The subject of tithing seems to push people's buttons, the favorite question (indicator of resistance) being, "Ten percent of the net income or ten percent of the gross?" Of course, our minds would prefer to voluntarily give up the lesser ten percent. However, Caesar and Uncle Sam take their chunk from the gross. You'll be surprised at how easy it becomes. In my comparatively short time as a tither, I've learned that no matter what my income level, I can always afford to give ten percent of my gross income to God's service. And much to my surprise, it always comes back greater in ways I'd never expect.

How do you let go of attachments? The same way that you let go of a moving rope. Completely. To hold on to that moving rope is to allow yourself to be dragged along by it. To hold on to that rope just a little, so that it slips through your hands even while you think you have some sort of control over the situation, is to invite rope burn. To hold on to the threads of a relationship that is no longer is to invite heartburn. We all have a choice: to nurture attachments by being curators of museums dedicated to maintaining some level of dependence on someone or something which is no longer part of our life, or like the child who is unattached to the toy house that he just demolished, we can pick up the pieces and build anew.

You are the dreamer,
dreaming up the waters.
You are the skater,
balanced on the narrow blade.

DOUG BENECKE
(FROM HIS SONG "INSIDE AND OUTSIDE")

KEITH'S DREAM

Keith called this morning to tell me of the dream he had last night. Keith's wife died from cancer a little less than a year ago. They'd been married twenty-eight years.

"Lon," he said excitedly, "I had this dream last night. It was so strange. I'm bothered by it. I can't figure it out. Doris [his wife] was in it. We were in the house, downstairs in the living room, and she was leaving, going out the door. It was like we were divorced, and now she was leaving me. I pleaded with her and started crying, 'Don't go. Don't go.' The next thing I know, I'm awake and crying."

"You woke up crying?" I asked.

"Yeah. She was leaving me, like in a divorce, and I plead with her, 'Don't go. Don't go,' and I wake up crying. What the hell was that all about?"

"Well, Keith," I offered, "it sounds like you were releasing some attachments to Doris. You two had been together quite awhile, right?"

"We were married twenty-eight years, but we'd known each other a few years before we married. Maybe thirty, thirty-one years."

"Okay. Let's say thirty years. That's long enough to know

someone, especially so intimately, that you become sort of entangled in each other's minds. You get to know someone so
well that you think how they would respond *before* you do
something, so that when you do something for yourself you
are still doing it in reference to the other person."

"You can say that again."

"When they are gone, suddenly you're back at the place
where you are thinking for just yourself. Yet, you've got those
memories in your mind which were important at one time, but
aren't so important anymore. Because . . ."

"Wait, Lon. Memories are important."

"Hold on a second, Keith. You're right. But let me finish.
They aren't so important now because it's just you again doing
for you on a day-to-day basis. You're no longer thinking, 'What
would she say? What would she do?' You're thinking primarily
about yourself, making those decisions which sustain you. Yet,
you do hold on to some memories, for instance, your trip to
Hawaii together, or the way she used to laugh. Right?"

"Right."

"I know that when I go through the Arboretum, I still think
of Nancy and how she enjoyed the flowers. But my point is,
gradually our conscious mind lets go of the day-to-day type
entanglements or attachments so that we can function more
clearly in our changed situation."

"Okay, I follow all of that. But what does it have to do with
my dream?"

"Dreams come from the subconscious mind. Dreaming is
the process our subconscious mind uses to flush out its stored
imagery, to do problem solving and to work through relationships, entanglements and attachments. At least that's the way
it works for me."

"I'll buy that."

"So, your dream was your subconscious mind's way of saying good-bye to Doris. It was you releasing attachment from a
deeper level of your being. It is similar to the process a person
goes through when they stop using an addicting substance.

The easy part is the physical elimination of the stuff from their systems. That takes from ten to fourteen days. But it takes from six to ten months to get it out of their minds, to eliminate the mind's needing to think that it needs the stuff in order to be.

"It's the same thing when we go through our grief process. The physical readjustment happens relatively quickly. But dealing with our mental and emotional attachments takes time. The first thing we have to do is accept that our wives are dead, and we will no longer be with them—at least not in this lifetime. We then go through our attachments, layer by layer, until we've cleared all the levels.

"It sounds as if your deeper self is acknowledging that Doris is gone. You didn't want to her to go, both in your dream and in reality, but she left. So, now you're starting to work on your subconscious level's attachments to Doris. Hang in there, you're doing fine. And of course, part of it is that just when you think you've cleared your attachments at one level and are ready to go on to the next, something happens which seems to put you right back where you started."

"Ain't that the truth," Keith said. "That happened to me last week. I was out driving. I was feeling pretty chipper. I'd had a good night's sleep, and I'd gotten my taxes done. I parked down by the lake and was watching the boats and listening to the radio. Then, Tony Bennett comes on singing, 'Because of You.' We liked that song. I started listening to the words. The next thing you know I have a lump in my throat, and I started bawling, tears streaming down my face—everything. And I've heard that song since, and . . . nothing. No tears, nothing. It's just another song to me. If that ain't the damnedest thing."

"It's happened like that for me too, Keith. It still does. I think I've cried myself out over something, eliminated some attachment, and it pops up again at some unexpected time, stops me in my tracks, and I think, 'Will this never end?' But then I remind myself that it's okay, let it go; better to clear it now than get sick over it later. So, I do, and then it's gone—like the last roll of thunder from a passing storm."

"Well, Lon, there is something to that. I do feel like I'm getting a handle on the situation. Last year, I used to cry for days and weeks. This year, I only cry for minutes."

VULNERABILITY AND
NEW RELATIONSHIPS

Grief is a process. Grief is not just the crying, the loneliness, the longing, the feeling of emptiness, the anger, the search for meaning—it is all of these and more. Grief is the process, the total process, that includes all of the above mentioned specifics, plus more, depending on who is grieving. We all go through grief at some time in our lives. We do it in different ways, which is understandable since we are all different in our expressions of life anyway. But we all go through grief.

For me, grief is the process of emptying out, of eliminating feelings, emotions, etc. It is like emptying a cup of stale coffee. I take the cup and pour the contents down the drain. It is my choice to watch the coffee as it bubbles and swirls into that orifice that leads under the city and into the ocean. It's my choice to even think about where it's going. If I wanted to, I could empty the cup drop by drop in order to minutely examine each aspect of the reddish brown colloidal suspension. However, I, like most people, dump it and forget about it. Once the cup is empty, however, we have a whole new ball game. This is the part that takes decision. This is the part that requires responsibility. This is the part that will determine what happens next. This part is absolutely necessary. This is the part that answers the question, "With what do I refill the cup?"

I could refill the empty cup with stale coffee; after all, it is familiar to me; I know what it is. Or I could refill the cup with fresh coffee. That too is familiar and in a way, safe. However, this cup of coffee will not be the same as the one I just dumped.

It might be worse. It might be better. Lord knows that no two cups of coffee are ever the same. Or I could refill the cup with herb tea (I know it's better for me) or fresh water or gasoline. All of these choices present themselves when the cup is empty and needing refilling. Some choices we dismiss automatically. Who wants to drink gasoline? Others are more of a challenge. For example, are we ready to go through caffeine withdrawal as a result of switching from coffee to herb teas? More than likely, we take the safe way out and refill the cup with more coffee—fresh, not stale.

I, like that cup, am being emptied of my old, stale emotions by the process called grief. That's why, when I'm grieving, I feel empty inside. That's why, after a good cry, I feel empty inside. How I refill my inner emptiness will determine the next part of my life. Granted, that "next part" could last only a few moments or a few years or even the rest of my life. In any event, how I fill my emptiness is a big responsibility—me being responsible to me for me.

This emptying out, this grieving process is a time of vulnerability. In past times of grief and vulnerability, I've allowed myself to be seduced into following someone else's belief system, even though I knew it wasn't mine; I've committed myself to employment situations that were ultimately self-destructive; or I've squandered my assets on shiny, shallow stuff. This time, I'm experiencing the deepest grief I've ever known. This time I'm feeling intense vulnerability that comes with having my heart broken—well, not so much broken as ripped out, torn apart, the parts spread out, reassembled and stuffed back into my chest. I feel as naked and exposed as a man being crucified must have felt. Yet, like the man being crucified, I can choose to look down to see the horror, disgust, delight and anguish reflected on the faces of people watching me die, or I can look up and follow the subtle color changes in the sky as the sunlight gets filtered by a passing wisp of cloud.

Now, as the emptiness, the longing, the desire for a new relationship gets stronger and stronger, I feel most vulnerable. I know that there is no way I can duplicate the relationship I had with Nancy. Yet, I need to have those gaps filled that she filled so well. To cut myself off from a new relationship with the thought that no one else can do me like she did is to make a gross mistake. It's true that our relationship was unique, one of a kind and very special. She was my first wife. However, I need to acknowledge that I, like that empty coffee cup, need to be refilled. I need a relationship in order to feel complete. The relationship I choose to get into requires me using my discrimination.

Do I want to be with someone who reminds me of Nancy? That would appear safe, yet, from what I've seen of others' experiences as they followed the road of being with someone who reminds them of their former spouse, that path is rocky and full of explosive devices because no two people are alike. And it is unfair to project a set of expectations on someone who cannot and will not fulfill them. Besides, it turns the specialness of the first relationship into an illusion, maybe even destroys it entirely.

Do I want to be with someone who has interests similar to Nancy's? That might give me more of the same, but with a new twist. Do I want someone entirely different? That, of course, is the challenge. That is the one that makes my palms sweat. That is the one that is scary. Being with someone entirely different will challenge me to grow. To be with her, not a shadow Nancy, will present me with situations I've never had to deal with before. That's what shakes me up the most. That's what threatens the protective shell I've put around my vulnerability. Fear of the unknown. That's what keeps me from putting a personal ad in the local paper. A challenge is an obstacle is an opportunity. That's what is outside my cave. That's what I need.

Knowing nothing shuts the iron gates;
the new love opens them.

The sound of the gates opening wakes
the beautiful woman asleep.

Kabir says: Fantastic! Don't let
a chance like this go by!

ROBERT BLY
THE KABIR BOOK

DATING AGAIN

My first ad in the singles personal classified was a complete flop. Zero response. The universe must have been reflecting back to me that my heart wasn't really in it, I really wasn't interested in starting a new relationship. After several months of writing and rewriting my ad, coupled with always managing to call in my latest attempt after the deadline so it wouldn't be taken, I gave up.

I fooled around with trying to write my ad for the better part of a year. Last month, like the month before, I sat down once again to try my luck at writing a personal ad. This time, the right words tumbled out onto the paper. I read them over, made a few changes and presto! I had my ad. I called my friend Larry, who had run an ad several months before and had received fifty responses, and read it to him. (I considered him my personal ad guru.) "Great," he said, "run it." So I did. I got twenty-four responses.

Last week, I met two of the women on the same day, one at lunch and the other at afternoon tea. That night I had a very powerful dream in which I dreamed of Nancy. Her face was as I remembered seeing her at the funeral home in Tijuana. Her body was full and vigorous, not emaciated as she was towards the end. She had on the new eyeglasses she had always intended to get. I called out to her in my dream, "Nancy, I really miss you a lot. I really miss you. Please don't let me confuse you; keep your energy where it is. I miss you, and I love you." I woke up crying.

I did not expect that dream that night. My subconscious must have been reacting to the energy stimulus of meeting the women by eliminating another layer of grief. Like I said, I wasn't expecting it. It shook me up; I was in a funk the next day from it. I should have called Keith for moral support. Instead, I chose to mope around. After awhile, though, I took time to listen to the observations I had given Keith and applied them to myself.

In so doing, I realized that the solid, loving relationship Nancy and I had had permeated all levels of my being. I was surprised the relationship had gotten as deep as it had as quickly as it had. After all, we were together for only four years. I thought a part of me would remain aloof, would not get intertwined in the relationship, would be my integrity, my "inner core" acting independently of all that was going on around me. Not so. I was in the relationship; I had given myself over to it, and it had returned my investment by filling me with a love I'd never known before.

In dreaming of Nancy after meeting the two women, I was acknowledging how much I needed her and the good loving relationship we had. I was also revealing my fear of doing it again; life would be so much simpler if we were still together. Later, I told some friends, using more macho words to cover my fears, that starting a new relationship is such a hassle.

In effect, a relationship is like a child—something you've created and invested yourself in, something that is a part of you, yet is its own separate entity with its own life independent from the lives of the people who sustain it, while at the same time being totally dependent on others for its sustenance.

Making a relationship work requires each partner giving 100 percent of themselves to their 50 percent of the relationship.

Losing a loved one also means losing the relationship you shared with them. Therefore, one's grief process also includes eliminating feelings about the relationship. Attachment to the relationship, in addition to attachment to one's lost loved one, complexifies the grief process even more. Now you have two major areas of attachment which contribute heavily to those feelings of loss and which need to be worked through.

Some men deal with their feelings of loss by leaping into marriage soon after the death of their spouse with the hope and intent of keeping the old relationship alive. Time proves the fallacy of such a notion as they look around two or three years later, after they've healed/gone through their grief, and seeing what they're in, they say, "What am I doing here?" They finally see the relationship they jumped into at a time when they were most vulnerable, and they want out. These are sad and lonely and unfair marriages.

Other men deal with the loss of their wives by shutting themselves away. They venture out only for necessities. Their vulnerability makes them easy prey for others and for their own minds. They live unhappily isolated in the present, while grasping for pleasant memories from the past.

There are times when I feel like I've become a hermit who would rather live in the past because the present is so frustrating. I have been deliberately reluctant to go into new relationships, even of the most superficial kind. I prefer to use my chosen semi-isolation to work through my grief process, actively integrating the transformational insights I've gleaned from contemporary and classical authors. I want my grief process to be a positive transformational event, so that I come out of it a winner, ready to move on with my life. And it is working, slowly and surely, as cleanly as the harpsichord music I like to play in the background as I type.

I think of Bach and his many children. I think of the intellectual satisfaction he must have felt after completing one of his compositions, proving once again that a tremendous amount of exploration can take place within very narrow confines.

I'm beginning to realize that my confines may be too narrow. My needs go beyond intellectual satisfaction and, to some extent, emotional satisfaction. I, like Fellini's uncle up in the tree, need a woman. I need a relationship with a woman. That is a good realization for me; it shows that I'm coming out of my "cave" (that place inside myself where I retreated to in order to recover from the shock and hurt I felt from Nancy's suffering and death). I'm opening the curtains of my apartment too to let the sunlight in.

Out there, outside my cave, are people, lots of people. At first, the vibrancy of all that life is overpowering. Yet if I'm to find my next "special woman," I must persevere. After all, I've decided to become a deuterogamist. That word, "deuterogamist," jumped out of the dictionary at me one day; a deuterogamist is one who has a second marriage after the death of the first spouse. That's the way Webster defines it, perhaps including a prejudice against divorce. Divorcees who marry again are not included in his strict definition. The Greeks, whose word it was in the first place, call it "second marriage," *deuteros* (second) plus *gamos* (marriage).

I leave my cave; I've had enough of shadows. I take shelter in the familiarity of the Danica support group. Then I venture further and find other groups which reflect my various interests. These groups offer me a transition place, a safe environment in which to begin integrating the results of my grief process into living a full life again back in society.

The groups have turned out to be more helpful than I first realized. They allow me to integrate my thoughts and feelings gradually and more thoroughly than I would in, let's say, the demands of a one-to-one relationship as in dating. Also, in the groups I gain practice in the art of social intercourse. I learn once again how to be with people who are busy being involved in life's activities.

I meet women in these groups. We get to know each other as people who share a common interest, instead of as possible mates checking out each other. We talk. Sometimes we talk superficially, other times deeply. Special relationships develop with both married and unmarried women. They become like my sisters, women I can talk with and learn from. It's like having family close by, instead of 3,000 miles away.

My "sisters" give me an understanding of what it is to be a woman dealing with today's issues. This helps me when I meet

other women, especially those I've chosen to check out. I feel
less awkward. I feel less vulnerable. I feel more confident. I feel
more alive.

I pray the Lord will continue to grant me the strength and
courage to accept what each day offers: the sunshine, the rain,
the opportunities, the challenges. I pray the Lord will continue
to grant me the strength and courage to let old attachments
pass. I pray the Lord will continue to grant me the strength and
courage to let resurrected love flow from me and new love flow
to me. Amen.

The process of growth, it seems, is the art of falling down. Growth is measured by the gentleness and awareness with which we once again pick ourselves up, the lightness with which we dust ourselves off, the openness with which we continue and take the next unknown step, beyond our edge, beyond our holding, into the remarkable mystery of being.

STEPHEN LEVINE
MEETINGS AT THE EDGE

CRYING

I need to cry. I've been needing to cry all day. The tears have stuck in my throat like a cold that won't go away. And they won't come out. Yet, everything I do, no matter what it is, has poked at the dam holding in my sorrow.

There is no rhyme nor reason for this. Little unrelated events somehow seem part of a pattern designed to illuminate (expose) my sorrow. Not that I'm trying to hide anything. There are days, even weeks, when I go about my merry way, dealing with the minutiae of my life, seeing Nancy's picture on my dresser and basically not thinking about anything except that which needs to be done. Then days like this one come on.

It's not so much depression as it is sadness, longing, the recognition of my grief, the remembrance of the reason for my grief. I want to cry, but it won't come out. Instead, I go through the activities of life as if in a fog. It's truly a wonder—no, a miracle—that on days like this one I have no traffic accidents.

In the restaurant, I wanted no communication with anyone. I went in, ate, paid and left. People walked by the table; I felt invisible. I didn't want to be seen. I went and hid in a movie. It was filmed in the Amish country near where I was raised. An act of supreme will kept me from heading east on the freeway after the movie and bagging this whole scene here in Seattle. I didn't even want to stop by my apartment and pick up my checkbook. Homesickness. Longing. Feeling the emptiness. Feeling the loneliness. Feeling the aloneness. Feeling in desperate need of a hug.

And needing to cry! I feel like a dammed stream. What keeps me from crying? Am I not yet full up enough to overflow into tears? Do I need to agonize some more, need to suffer inside some more in order to build up a sufficient quantity of sadness which will burst through the dam and come out as tears? Is this the way a man cries?

Women seem to cry at the drop of a hat. There doesn't seem to be any accumulation of stuff before the women in my life have cried. On the other hand, the men in my life (myself included) seem to cry only after there is an accumulation of negative events. Then the proverbial straw that breaks the camel's back starts the tears flowing. For myself, I've given myself permission over and over to cry, to let it out, to eliminate my grief. My understanding of why people cry completely satisfies my mind. Crying is one of the forms of bodily eliminations; crying allows us to eliminate emotions and unacted upon feelings from our bodies, where they would otherwise be stored. It's not as if I am trying to hold back the tears. I know, feel, understand, believe that it is right for me to cry, that it is okay for me to cry, that there is nothing wrong or unmanly about crying, that crying is an integral part of the human experience. So, why am I not crying?

Has social conditioning created a monitor in me who stops the tears from flowing and says, "MEN DON'T CRY!?" If so, I don't hear him. I don't even feel him. Is the conditioning so subtle and deep that even when my head, heart and hands say, "Go for it," I can't?

Or is it biological? I recently read somewhere that researchers have found that men's and women's tears have different chemical compositions. Maybe men aren't designed and built to cry as often as women. Maybe men have a larger storage capacity for sadness. Maybe the current social training we have, that men aren't supposed to cry, was originally that men aren't supposed to cry as frequently as women because they don't have to, that frequent crying is the womanly way. I honestly don't know.

The liberations of the past decade have changed men. We no

longer see ourselves in the same light as before. We are acknowledging that men are capable of being more and doing more than ever before. John Lennon, for example, showed us that a man can stay home and raise a child; his final years were dedicated to raising his son, Sean. Our brothers, the Vietnam vets we see weeping openly at the Vietnam war memorial in Washington, D.C., are showing us that men do cry, that men need to cry to wash away the pain of losing someone they love.

Men cry like men. Some tears flow. There may or may not be some sounds accompanying the tears. There may or may not be some movement. From my own experience of recent months, tears have flowed spontaneously, but very few tears at any one time. I've not made much sound when I cried, and my only movement was to wipe my eyes. Only once, soon after Nancy died, did I get into a major cry. I remember I wailed into a pillow and beat on the mattress with my fists. I don't remember how long it lasted. But it seemed to be over as quickly as it came.

I feel as if I need to do that now. Yet nothing happens. No tears flow, no sense of release. I sit here typing with a lump in my throat. And that's as far as I've gotten with it all day.

Maybe I'm taking this too seriously, going through all this analysis over why I'm not able to cry right now. Perhaps I need to be more gentle with myself, to do as Stephen Levine says and dust myself off lightly. A light, loving touch is often more powerful in restoring balance and harmony than is a forceful approach. It's time to remember that one cannot push the river. Whatever happens, happens. There is no way to force the issue. When tears are ready to flow, they will flow. And when they do, I will cry like a man.

Fathers, don't be ashamed to let your sons see you cry.

DANAAN PERRY

TIM MONAGHAN'S
MEMORIAL SERVICE

Tim and I met in a pizza parlor where we shared a table. He introduced me to his pride and joy, his daughter, Elena, and he bought me a Guinness. We talked about everything. What we didn't cover in that first conversation, we covered in subsequent ones. Even in our last conversation, which took place under the birch trees outside of the hospice one week before he died from cancer, we discussed everything.

Well, not quite everything. The closer Tim got to death, the more he got to his essence. The things he said were pearls, and I felt like a swine, sitting there in awe of the clarity of his vision in spite of one glass eye and an expanding brain tumor diminishing his other eye's sight.

He was going through his grief. He was letting go of his attachments. He acknowledged that his biggest attachment was to Elena. She was five. He loved her tremendously.

As he talked, his eloquence conveyed part of what a man's grief often includes, loving concern for others. In Tim's case, it was his concern for the children, especially Elena. He was concerned for his daughter's growing up in a world in which people with power high-handedly abuse the people they supposedly serve and represent by continually keeping everyone stressed out with threats of nuclear obliteration. Tim was concerned that this state of constant fear and stress would generate so much ill will among people that the beautiful, pure love he saw manifesting in his daughter would not have a chance to blossom. He was sad that love has to struggle to stay alive, while hate has free rein to walk all over every one and every thing. He looked at me with a wistful sadness and said, "I'm a taxi driver by choice because I do not want to make enough money to have to pay taxes and support the government's madness. It's *the* government. It's not even our government anymore."

Tim died on Tuesday. He was almost 35. His funeral was the following Sunday. The church was packed. The service consisted of family and friends paying tribute to a man who had affected many lives. Elena and her friends from her pre-school class sang "Somewhere over the Rainbow."

Tim's funeral was the first funeral I had attended since Nancy died. As I sat there listening to the music, I felt a huge wave of grief come over me. I felt agitated, like I wanted to get up and leave the room, and peaceful at the same time. Even though Tim and I were brothers in the spirit, the grief that was sweeping through me seemed disproportionately too intense for the situation. I sat back in the pew and gave myself over to the grief. I let go, and the tears, the welcome tears, began to flow. I felt enveloped by a deep, almost shock-like state. And I cried some more. Although I felt sad about Tim's death, I recognized that this deep release was not about him. This was for Nancy.

At long last, I was having the deep release of sadness and sense of loss that I had needed for quite awhile. For well over a year and a half, I had been holding in all the deep sadness I felt for Nancy's death that I wanted/needed to eliminate at her funeral, but couldn't because I was coordinating her funeral, making arrangements, meeting guests, helping arrange flowers and chairs, and on and on. I was so busy and going through so much inner turmoil, that I didn't have the opportunity to just sit back and let it all out.

At Tim's funeral, I was totally receptive, sitting there listening to the music, listening to the words, getting lost in the clouds painted on the wall behind the altar, hearing the sobbing around me, feeling the sadness around me, and letting it all help me to let go and go through more layers, deep layers, of my grief over the death of my beloved wife, Nancy.

The grief process is complex. It is not a one-shot deal. It is more like an onion; after you go through one layer, there is another and another and another. We don't get into the next layer until we are ready for it. Sometimes we don't know we are ready, and the next layer comes as a surprise—much as it did for me at Tim's funeral. Sometimes there are so many layers that the grief seems endless. One could easily become depressed from all the crying and sorrow (grief) that one is going through. This secondary depression could become a problem, as it adds another layer to the already existing layers of emotional elimination that are taking place in the grief process. Rather than becoming distracted by this secondary depression and thinking that the grief will go on forever, try considering the secondary depression as an indicator that you have gone through one layer and have just encountered another. That way you can get a sense of the flow of the process called grief. By accepting grief as a process, grief becomes easier to take/to have/to do. It ain't easy, but it is survivable. More than that, by understanding grief as a process, you can not only survive it, you can also utilize it for your own positive growth. You become the observer and monitor (the seer) of the process, rather than its victim.

I'm glad that Tim's funeral let me get out that deep, long-held sorrow. I feel a lot lighter; I am no longer carrying around some undefined weight inside. I'm sure Tim didn't mind me utilizing his funeral to unload my sadness. He was that kind of guy.

1986

SEX, SUCCESS AND GOING TO THE DENTIST

I hate going to the dentist. My hate affair with dentists began when I was eight years old. Mom took me to a dentist who didn't like what he was doing. His business principles were simple: charge people twice for the same job. First you would get a temporary filling, then you would return a few weeks later and get a permanent filling for the same cavity. Each filling required its own drilling and re-drilling. His equipment was World War II military surplus, his training was U.S. Army, and his eyes—when he wasn't staring in my mouth—always seemed to be somewhere else. His smile looked like something he practiced in front of a mirror—always the same, affecting only that part of his face between his nose and chin. And he always gave me a sugar-sweetened lollipop before I left his office. He knew how to keep his customers coming back for more.

I hated him. I feared him. I'd sit in his chair, too terrified to move. I quickly learned that it did no good to protest. The alternative to a Saturday morning's agony (sometimes all day if I got those mouth-numbing shots) was a mouth full of decayed, rotting teeth. Or worse—braces! Who wanted that!?! To survive my time in the chair, I'd get completely tense, wrap my hands tightly around the chair handle supports, clamp my eyes shut so I wouldn't see the diabolical instruments he was sticking in my mouth and think of nothing. I certainly did not want to imagine what he was doing. Meanwhile, my head vibrated to the slow, dull whacks of his drill as he chipped away bits of my teeth.

Only once did I panic, when his over-heated drill filled my head with the odor of burning tooth. I remember he liberally sprayed my mouth with water and ordered me to spit out into the little gurgling sink next to the chair. He gave me (and his drill) a few minutes to cool down before starting again.

As a reaction to the abusive approach of my childhood dentist, I have learned to take care of my teeth. Like Shirley MacLaine's Russian lover, I too have a Water Pik. I floss regularly, brush carefully and massage my gums, so I usually need no work done.

Recently, I received a notice from a new dental practice opening in my neighborhood—an introductory exam with x-rays and cleaning for only $1.00, a deal I could not refuse. As I sat in his office waiting my turn, my old apprehensions reappeared. To defuse them, I began reading a magazine. It may have been *OMNI* or *Psychology Today* or even *Esquire*. I don't remember which.

The dentist turned out to be a compassionate man who took time to teach me how to relax in the chair before he began to work. His state-of-the-art equipment and techniques were excellent. For the first time in my life, I felt comfortable enough to open my eyes while the dentist worked on me. He asked if I would like a mirror in order to see what he was doing. I said, "Yes."

Getting back to the magazine, I had been reading an article which said that a man's sex drive increases with his status and success. It gave statistical evidence correlating perceived status and sexual performance. It got me thinking about the alpha male elk I had seen on a public TV show the night before. The alpha male is the one who battles and beats all challengers; he then gets to hump all the females.

I thought about my own life and how, for most of the past two years, I have been seeing myself on a low rung of life's ladder—as someone who has lost both love and time during a period of one's life that is normally used to acquire and solidify one's position in society. I have also not had much interest in sex. The hornies and the drive have been there, but (to paraphrase Rhett Butler) frankly, I didn't give a damn. It has only been during the past few months that I have achieved a level of success and have been involved in a sexual relationship.

My success has come in the stock market, parlaying insurance payments (which took a year's worth of phone calls and letters to clear up) into a profitable investment. I'm once again managing an apartment complex (a smaller one this time) which provides living space and time to write, evaluate and rebuild. I know I must have some status in the world, for every week I receive an offer to subscribe to some magazine or some investors' information service or some credit card. Even junk mail has its positive side: someone, somewhere, knows and appreciates that I exist.

As far as sex goes, my most recent relationship opened up another layer in my seemingly endless grief process. It was wonderful to be with a woman again, and it opened a Pandora's box of feelings.

It started simply enough. We met at a party and hit it off immediately. Soon after, we were lovers. Everything in our relationship was flowing smoothly. After awhile, though, I found I could not perform as well sexually with her as I had with Nancy and others. At first I thought I was losing it—the result of getting older. I talked with my male friends and learned that age has nothing to do with it. I thought it must be her; she's not doing what I need to get excited. But that wasn't true; just seeing her was a turn-on.

I accepted the problem I was having as being my own and began examining what I was doing that caused me to lose my sexual excitement when we were together. Using the *I Ching* expression, "No blame," I came to a compassionate understanding. During our love-play, we would get each other excited. But when I fondled her breasts, I lost my excitement. As I said before, I am a tactilely oriented person. I sense (and remember) through my hands. She had had silicon implants for cosmetic purposes. To me, her breasts felt exactly like Nancy's tumor-swollen breast—much like what you feel when you press your finger against the outside of your cheek while your tongue is pushing against it from the inside.

I decided to stop seeing her. We could not discuss the situation without inadvertently saying things which hurt each other. Also, our being together opened my Pandora's box of feelings regarding the cancer's intrusion into Nancy's and my sexual life. I felt it was better to not explore these feelings in this particular relationship.

Pandora, in Greek mythology, was the first mortal woman created in heaven by the gods and was sent to Earth by Zeus to punish (perhaps a more appropriate word would be vex) Prometheus for giving fire to man. Pandora, in her curiosity, opened a closed container (a box or jar, depending on your source text), thus releasing all the ills and plagues that mankind is subject to. In a less sexist version of the Pandora myth, the box contains blessings from the gods. In either version, the plagues or blessings all escape, with the only thing remaining in the box being Hope.

In my Pandora's box, I found deep sadness, fear and pain. First was the deep sadness which Nancy and I had shared as our decreasing physical intimacy reflected her increasing pain and sense of finality. There was my sad remembrance of our last precious moments together as we said what became our final good-byes. I found a feeling of irony in that of all the women I have known, the one I married died. I found fear of loving another woman who will die on me too soon. (I don't want to go through the pain and trauma again, at least not for a long, long time.) I found reticence over getting into a committed relationship. (Smokey Robinson's song "You Better Shop Around" plays softly in the background of my mind.) I found the pain of disappointment at how my life is going and envy of other men who have jobs and relationships which keep their lives in balance. I even found envy of older men who married young, raised a family, whose wives were the only women they had ever known, and who lost their spouses at the "normal" time—in their late sixties or older. And at the bottom, I find hope—hope that all the bits and pieces of my life will fit together again.

I think about the helpful talks I've had with my good buddy, Barney, and wonder why we men—with the exception of the one or two solid male friendships we develop during our lives—choose to connect with each other only in the areas of competition, criticism and war. (The only time I saw my childhood dentist's eyes sparkle was when he proudly showed me a picture of his U.S. Army officers graduating class. "Can you find me?" he asked as I studied the rows of uniformed men.) Is it because we have not been taught how to be with other men in supportive ways? If that's the case, the only ways left to relate are either to view each other as threats or to ignore each other completely.

Perhaps a lot of it has to do with the pattern in which we were raised: Mom was there providing caring support during the days, and Dad was there in the evenings (when he was tired from a day's work) and on the weekends (when there were chores to be done). We were taught to look to women for sustained, caring support, a lesson we men perpetuate. But we men need to realize that women cannot be our sole source of caring support. That is part of what Women's Liberation is all about.

Slowly but surely we are learning to stop projecting all of our needs onto women only. Slowly but surely we are learning to be present completely with each other as men. Where are we learning this? In men's support groups, in Vietnam vets' support groups and in the work place where the mentor system is used. (Mentor, in Greek legend, was the loyal friend and wise adviser of Odysseus [Ulysses], and teacher and guardian of Odysseus' son, Telemachus.) In the movie *Star Wars*, Ben is Luke Skywalker's mentor who encourages Luke to go with his feelings while teaching him needed skills.

But, what does this have to do with me? Well, for example, I found in talking with supportive men that I got clear about my hang-up regarding silicon-implanted breasts—something I could not do when talking with my women friends, as they became defensive and argumentative. I'm finding within the sanctity of caring relationships with men, that I can freely explore the lessons of my grief process.

There is something about having been to the edge with Nancy, having seen death, that has changed my perspective on life. I now have a much broader view and a narrower view.

The broader view gives an overview of the human experience and establishes priorities. For example, death itself is no longer that vague thing waiting at the end of a long and winding road, but rather a clear event only a breath away. The priority becomes to make the most of the moment each breath makes possible. Life becomes more precious and less precarious. Life is a miracle which does not need to expend itself on erecting barriers against its own creations. The fear of death gets supplanted by the joy of living. Subscribing to systems of thought offering protection from elaborate death-dealing "others" which the systems themselves have created is no longer seen as one of life's necessities. It has all become less complicated. The linear string of a single life becomes the cyclical flow of life in general. All religions reveal their commonality. Everything fits together. I feel peace in my heart.

I also feel a narrowing of my vision of who I am, what I want to be doing and who I want to be doing it with. I am more conscious of the women I choose to be with. I do not want to intentionally re-create an experience which devastated me.

Nancy's death, although the most intense, was not the first death of a woman I cared for. As an undergraduate, I loved a girl who committed suicide soon after we started dating. I never found out why or knew anyone who did. While studying at San Francisco State College, I was infatuated with a girl who (I found out two years later when I returned to the city) had died of Hodgkin's disease during my absence. Each death took something out of me and filled me with a desire to give more of myself to the next relationship.

In my narrower vision, I recognize myself as being an intensely sensual and sexual being. I cannot deny my sexuality. It did not die when Nancy died. I found that out a few days after I returned from Mexico with Nancy's ashes. A woman I'd known for over a year telephoned. (We'd worked together at the time I was working three jobs.) "How are you?" she asked. "What are you doing?"

"I'm totally freaked," I said, glad to have someone to talk with. "I'm sitting here looking at all our stuff. I've got to get it out of here in the next ten days. I found a mini-warehouse storage locker over in Ballard for some of the stuff. The rest is for sale. I'm having a garage sale this weekend, so I'm busy sorting, packing and pricing. When I'm not doing that, I'm asleep. Or else I'm sitting, staring at the bookcase in total, tear-streaked shock."

"Would you like me to come over and help?" she asked. "I'm good at pricing things."

"Gladly," I said. "I need someone to talk to." An hour later, she arrived.

As promised, she did know how to price things. And she was not pushy when I would stop working and stare out the window. After dinner, we worked some more, pricing and packing. "I've got to be going," she said.

"Thanks for coming over," I said. We hugged. She felt good, full of life, vibrant. I didn't want to let go. She didn't either. We spent the night together having passionately abandoned sex. I felt wonderful. Ours was the first unrestrained physical release I had had in well over six months.

Early the next morning, I walked her to her car. We met an elderly resident of the building who looked at me as if I had committed the worst possible sin. I went back to bed, my body still tingling and my mind filled with thoughts of what Clark Gable must have gone through when he learned that his wife, Carole Lombard, had died in a plane crash on the same night he was in the sack with another actress. (That's from a fictionalized biography film I saw about Clark Gable and may not be historically accurate. Still it presented me with a moral bone to chew on.)

Did I do something wrong? Am I supposed to feel guilt for what I've done? I don't feel any. I feel no sense of shame. I take responsibility for what I did. Actually, I'm glad it happened; getting lost in sensual pleasure pulled me out of my shock-induced thought rut and reconnected me to my body and my physical presence in the world. I have no regrets.

Our affair was over quickly. She saw she was not getting what she wanted—a committed relationship, and I saw I needed to withdraw into my self to work through my grief. We parted amicably.

Now it's two years later, and my interest in sexual relations has renewed itself. But my view of sex has narrowed; I no longer view it as something to be done with as many different partners as possible. My Swinging Sixties "free love" attitude has changed. Sexual relations involve more than giving and receiving physical pleasure. Sex is a very intimate, sensitive thing which also includes in itself emotional involvement and spiritual connection. Yet, I let the physical aspects influence my most recent relationship. Perhaps I have not evolved as far as I sometimes think I have. I still get turned on by the physical aspects of sex. And yet, I know at some level (undoubtedly the spiritual) that sex can be the ultimate expression of a relationship (as it was with Nancy), not the relationship itself.

At the spiritual level, where everything ultimately ends up anyway, souls continually bathe in the ocean of energy known as God's Love. (As Dr. Frank Alper, noted author of *Exploring Atlantis*, says, "God always wins.") As souls manifest in physical bodies, they get separated from the source. Well, not totally separated, it just feels like separation. A soul goes from "skinny dipping" in God's Love to being encased in a suit of muscle and bone. However, the connection to God is always there; the door is always ready to open to us embodied souls; all we have to do is knock.

Some of us knock on God's door through such spiritual

practices as meditation or chanting. Others find a refreshing immersion in the river of life through *seva*, selfless service to others, as exemplified by Mother Teresa. Still others reconnect with God through the intense spiritual experience of Holy Communion. We all have our ways, provided we choose/ remember/learn to use them.

Some of us become so involved with our encapsulation devices (our bodies) and the environment in which they operate that we forget (or choose not to remember) how this all actually works.

Yet all souls seek at some level the energy hit of God's Love. When one soul's experience of God's Love is not as intense as the soul would like it to be, given the limiting effect of the human body, the soul seeks another soul with whom to unite in order to create a synergistic multiplication which will, hopefully, be closer to the intensity each soul has nostalgic longing for from his/her "skinny dipping" days.

Sex is the closest thing to soul union that two embodied souls can share, given the limitations caused by their bodies being in the way. Yet, on the physical plane, sex is necessary for reproduction of the species and to help keep bodies feeling good.

In yoga, which also helps keep bodies feeling good, one uses exercises and meditations to harmonize the activity of one's chakras,[1] so they are all spinning at their proper frequencies, complementing each other rather than competing with each other.

In terms of sex, the chakras from the heart upward are for making a spiritual union. The lower chakras operate more on

---

1   Chakras are spinning energy centers found in the human body. They are located along the ultrasonic core (roughly, the spinal column) where they transmute very high frequency cosmic energy into sustaining life energy. There are seven chakras; starting from the bottom, they are: (1) earth chakra, in the region of the bowels; (2) water chakra, in the pelvic basin; (3) fire chakra, at the solar plexus; (4) air chakra (also called heart chakra), in the chest; (5) ether chakra, in the throat; (6) third eye chakra, near the pineal gland, and (7) crown chakra, at the top of the head.

the physical level. According to Asha Praver, teacher and co-minister of the Fellowship of Inner Communion in Palo Alto, California, and a student of Sri Kriyananda, the art of making sex spiritual is to make it nonphysical. She suggests that sex may still involve our physical bodies, but by focusing our attention on our hearts, as in opening our hearts to our partner, instead of on our desire for personal gratification, sex can become more and more a spiritual experience.

In my narrower view, I'm learning more about love too. For instance, a man has sex with a partner, likes it and goes for the security of continuing having sex with that same partner. He calls this love. A woman wants security in a committed relationship; she shares sex with a partner in order to cement the relationship. She calls this love. According to Jesus, God is love. According to my teacher, unqualified acceptance is love. Dr. Gerald G. Jampolsky wrote a best-selling book titled *Love is Letting Go of Fear*. I'm beginning to believe that love is the word we use when we can't think of any other label for the feeling of blissful completion we experience when we get beyond our ego selves.

I'm also beginning to accept that the lover I'm looking for is really inside of me in the form of my inner feminine or *anima* (in the Jungian sense) or goddess (in the mythical sense). John A. Sanford, a Jungian analyst and Episcopalian priest, recently (1980) wrote a book titled *The Invisible Partners: How the Male and Female in Each of Us Affects Our Relationships*. In it, he demonstrates how the feminine part of a man and the masculine part of a woman are the invisible partners in any male-female relationship. I'm finding his book (and the extensive bibliography he includes) very helpful in moving through to my next layer. Little did I know when I started my venture into the grief process that it would lead me to myself via all the notions, opinions, fallacies, ideas and prejudices of my mind.

Dr. Randolph Stone supports John Sanford's thesis with graphic depictions of the masculine and feminine energy patterns found in all human bodies. The Charts, as they are called, are found in *The Wireless Anatomy of Man,* one of several books Dr. Stone wrote concerning Polarity Therapy.[1]

Chart No. 11 depicts the masculine energy pattern as two interlaced triangles, looking like a stretched out, not quite Star of David, reaching from the eyes to the pubic area. Masculine energy is our outgoing energy, our energy which moves both our bodies and things external to our bodies. It is functional energy (energy applied to perform a function). It is left brain, logical, systematic. The symbol for male (a circle with an arrow projecting out from the circle at an angle ♂) depicts the out-goingness of masculine energy (the arrow leaving the circle).

Dr. Stone ties masculine energy to the Fire Principle, one of three elemental Principles which activate life in the human body. The other Principles are Water (feminine) and Air (neu-ter). The Fire Principle is one of action and motivation, as in the saying, "If you want someone to do something, you'd better build a fire under them."

In astrology, three of the twelve signs are called fire signs. They are: Aries, Leo and Sagittarius. The other nine signs are grouped equally as water, air and earth signs. These groupings are not arbitrary; they are based on placing the signs in a circle in their usual sequence and drawing equilateral triangles among them. The signs connected by being at the corners of the same triangle form a group. Each of the twelve signs is as-signed a specific part of the human body which the sign then rules, in the sense that similar things attract each other, like attracts like.

Aries is the constellation of the ram. Rams, as we know, de-rive a peculiar satisfaction from banging their heads against walls, trees, other rams, anything. Aries rules the head. Don't you know someone born in April (actually March 21 to April 20) who is always celebrating life? Or is a hot-head?

1   Polarity Therapy is the energy-balancing system evolved by Dr. Randolph Stone during the 1950s. Based on the Ayurvedic health and medical system of ancient India and on other non-chemical health maintenance systems used by various cultures for thousands of years, Polarity Therapy combines non-strenuous exercises, hands-on manipulations and dietary awareness to help people take care of their own bodies.

Leo, the lion, rules the heart (remember Richard the Lion-Hearted?) and solar plexus, the little sun in the center of our bodies which acts like a brain supervising the fire of digestion. Dr. Stone warns against drinking ice water with meals, as it will cool the digestive organs to the point where they won't work properly, thus food becomes incompletely digested and begins to putrify in one's system. On the other hand, too much fire can manifest as—are you ready for this?—heartburn.

Sagittarius, of the three fire signs, best depicts Dr. Stone's Fire Principle as the attribute of masculine energy. Sagittarius is the centaur—half man and half horse. Sagittarius rules the thighs. The thighs continue the line of energy pattern established by the inverted triangle in Chart No. 11.

The man half of the centaur (a man's torso, shoulders, arms, neck and head coming out of the horse's body just in front of the forelegs where the horse's neck would normally be rooted) is holding a bow and arrow. When the man part, with his ability to reason, is in control, the arrow is aimed carefully and upon release, finds its target. The potent energy force of the arrow is sent into the world with discrimination. However, when the horse half of the centaur (the body and four legs of a horse) is in control, the arrows fly indiscriminately in all directions as the animal need for movement provides the archer with an unstable platform from which to shoot.

Reason (left brain) becomes the tool with which we exercise responsibility in our application of masculine, outgoing energy. Allowing our animal urges to guide our outgoing energy often results in things and/or situations and/or relationships which are not in our best possible interests.

Feminine energy, on the other hand, is receptive, intuitive, right brain, artistic. It deals with form, as in the form which makes possible/is a reflection of function. (Perhaps this is why we refer to ships as "she.") Feminine energy is the target which an arrow needs to find in order to satisfy its function as an arrow. The sign for female is a circle with a cruciform extending from the base arc of the circle ♀. Take the cruciform apart by splitting lengthwise the two lines which form the cross, and you have four right-angled arrow heads coming together at a common center from four different directions, from North, East, South and West; or if you prefer, from the four corners of the globe or from the four winds of the medicine wheel.

Feminine energy, as depicted in Charts Number 9 and 10 in Dr. Stone's *The Wireless Anatomy of Man*, is patterned like a five-pointed star. Its top point is placed at the throat, and its two bottom points rest on each hip.

Feminine energy is like the Water Principle, which, as Dr. Stone says in *Energy: The Vital Polarity in the Healing Art*, "convey[s] the vital energies as well as the emotional impulses in man." Water deals with cycles (rain to ocean to vapor to rain), with ebb and flow (like the tides, affected by the moon, the feminine receiver of the masculine sun's light), with emotions (the washing out of feelings), nurturing (witness the vitalizing effect of spring rain), and form (witness the actions of Water and her little sister, Air, as they sculpt and shape the landscape). In astrology, the water signs are Pisces, Scorpio and Cancer.

Pisces, the fish, rules the feet, those parts of our bodies which are in almost constant contact with the first of the two most important forms in our lives, our planet, Mother Earth. The feet, according to Reflexology, are maps of the other important form in our lives, our bodies. By maps, I mean that every organ and gland and the spinal column has a nerve ending in our feet. The nerve endings occur on the soles of our feet in proportion to where the organs appear in our bodies; the eyes are 'in' the base of the second and third toe, the sacrum (the base of the spinal column) is 'in' the heel, and the digestive organs (which are in the middle of our torso) are 'in' the middle of the feet. In Reflexology, as in Polarity Therapy, manipulation of the soles of the feet has an effect on the parts of the body upstream from the specific areas manipulated. The Piscean effect in our lives is one of harmony and smooth sailing/swimming/walking/dancing—until we think about it. When we stop to think which foot comes first, we stumble. When we take a moment to analyze the angle of the sail versus the angle of the rudder, we lose the balance between wind and water. Pisces fly by the seat of their pants. At least that's the way it's been for this Pisces.

Scorpio, the scorpion, rules the genitals and reproductive areas. With these, the human species reproduces its physical form. The scorpion, with its stinger and claws, also represents impermanence. The claws take things apart, specifically the little bodies on which the scorpion feeds. The stinger, with its unpredictable, lightning-quick jabs, deals out sudden death. In the pantheon of Tibetan Buddhist demigods, Kali celebrates impermanence by dancing on a corpse, while a necklace strung with human skulls swings from her neck. Scorpio creates a form which cannot last.

Cancer, the crab, rules the chest and breasts. It is the nurturing aspect of feminine energy, as exemplified by the breast-feeding mother. Cancer, the astrological sign, influences the home; the crab takes his house (his shell) with him wherever he goes. Do you know any Cancer people (June 21 to July 20)? Would you say they tend to be homebodies concerned with the welfare of their families? Cancer's essence is metamorphosis, just as a crab changes his "house" to accommodate his expansion. Emotion is a form of metamorphosis, changing feelings from perceptions to eliminations.

For the most part, crabs move sideways as they walk around the bottom of their watery world. They trust their sense of touch to guide them over the uneven surface. In Cancer people, the positive expression of this feature is called tact; the negative expression can be circumspection and deliberate indirection in their dealings with others and themselves.

All the water signs operate in the realm of feelings and emotions. But, they differ in their relationship to this realm. On one hand, Scorpio tends to intensify feelings by focusing the energy of the feelings into specific actions. On the other hand, Pisces swim around in an ocean of feelings and, like the ocean, contain within themselves a depth and vastness of feelings which are not always expressed. However, it falls to Cancer, who is sensitive to the entire range of feelings and emotions, to process the wide variety of feeling experience.

It seems no accident that the major disease confronting mankind is called cancer. Using esoteric interpretation, cancer (the disease) can be viewed as the result of emotional stagnation. (Emotions are an aspect of the Water Principle. Crabs live in sluggish backwaters, not in swiftly-moving, self-cleaning mainstreams). Tissue degeneration in cancer is accelerated by the over-consumption of dead, refined and processed foods. (Crabs are scavengers; they eat the remains which fall to the floor of their water world.)

Nancy's cancer manifested first in her breast. I know she had a lot of unresolved emotional issues. She was one of many women who find their lives distorted by unrealistic expectations resulting from an upbringing in which masculine and feminine energies in each of the parents (and in the couple relationship which the parents created) were out of balance. Lest you feminists misread me, I am not talking about the so-called balance of sexual stereotype role playing. I am talking about the balance obtained when a human being accepts and embraces the masculine and feminine energies within each one of us and utilizes to the full the information these energies present.

My new dentist presents a much more balanced use of his energies than did my childhood dentist. My new dentist is sensitive to my needs, caring about how he is doing what he is doing and straightforward in doing what needs to be done. I like him. I have no qualms about ever going back to him should I need some dental work.

For myself, I am peacefully accepting my own feminine, receptive, intuitive, nurturing qualities. I recognize that by accepting and loving my *anima*, my inner goddess, I will allow for a more harmonious next relationship (hopefully) because I won't be expecting her to be what I thought I needed to come from the outside, that which is actually inside of me.

As I look again at Dr. Stone's Chart No. 10, the five-pointed star pattern of feminine energy, I am struck by the position of the top point. It rests at the throat, the etheric center. Etheric energy rules space, openness, communications and grief. Interesting how ancient wisdom fits together.

Your thoughts and actions are only a set of mental habits in a state of flux as you evolve from stage to stage of your life's growth.

KEN KEYES, JR.
THE HUNDREDTH MONKEY

GRIEF THE HEALER

I know I've said this before, and I'm going to say it again because to me, the most important thing to remember about grief is that it is a process. The grief process is a flow of frequently dissimilar feelings and actions whose unifying element is their common source. The feelings and actions come out as a result of our suffering the pain of complete separation from someone we love. All that we feel and do is our grief. Our grief is the *Gestalt* in which healing takes place. The grief process is the facilitator of the healing.

Our bodies are marvelous in that they can heal themselves. We have all seen a cut or scratch heal in just a matter of days. Our minds can heal themselves too, although it takes longer because of the unlearning and relearning we need to go through. There was an axiom we followed in a drug abuse treatment program I worked with. It went, "It takes ten days for the body to become physically clean of the addictive substance and six months for the mind to let go of its behavioral patterns regarding the substance."

Like the drug dependent person going through his or her withdrawals, we who are going through grief have to confront and accept those many parts of ourselves which are each, in their own unique yet painful way, eliminating a deeply ingrained dependency on our relationship with our now departed loved one. Each aspect—be it anger, fear, frustration, guilt, longing, emptiness, loneliness, relief, shock, unusual behavior, etc.—has to be gone through and eliminated in order to complete the grief process. Only in completion does one get healed. On the other hand, attachment to one or more of the aspects stops the flow of the process. One gets stuck in one's own grief and doesn't get healed.

I know a rather unhappy lady whose husband committed suicide in a spectacular fashion nearly five years ago. She is still angry with him for doing what he did. She has a list of reasons for being angry which she thinks justifies her continued anger. Unfortunately, her holding on to her anger with him keeps her stuck in the grief process, which makes her even angrier because her grief never ends. Yet all she has to do is let go of her anger, watch it do its dance instead of being it doing the dancing and forgive him for doing what he did. This would move her along to the next step (whatever it is) in the flow of her grief process and hopefully reopen her heart to love and happiness. It's easier said than done, yet it can be done.

While going through my own grief process, I received a lesson on what was happening to me in, of all places, a car wash. I have always liked to sit inside the car and watch the water and brushes. This time, as I rode through the car wash, spray hammered the roof, and my car shook and rattled as it bounced through the wild, whirly tunnel. I felt my stomach tighten. Then came the lesson. If I allowed my apprehension to become fear, I would have gotten caught by the process. However, if I allowed myself to sit back and relax and recognize that the car will bounce around if I'm uptight about it or not (because its bouncing is part of the process of the car getting clean in this particular car wash machine), then I can enjoy the ride. So, I relaxed, experienced the process of the car getting washed, experienced my own reactions without becoming my reactions (i.e., acting out my feelings) and ended up feeling good about both my car and myself.

I applied this lesson to my own grief process, and it worked. I watched my feelings as they came up, and I did not become them. I felt pain, hurt, deep sorrow, and did not become them. I cried and eliminated emotions in other ways and did not become that which I eliminated. I took care of myself, as does anyone who is out of sorts and wants to get beyond it. Only this time, healing took place through the power of the grief process, not through medication.

I've been fortunate to meet people who have taken the chance/used the opportunity to go through their complete grief. One in particular, a woman named Sally, told me how she used to fear the hurt of loneliness after her husband died. She said, "I used to sit home and just cry my eyes out from fear of being alone. Then one time, I looked around and said to myself, 'This is silly. I already am alone. What have I got to be afraid of?' I sniffled a little more and then stopped. I still remember how good I felt after I was done. Oh, sure, I miss him," she continued, "but who can catch a shadow? Besides," she said while watching her employee bring in a stack of mail, "who has the time?"

If you are going through grief, let me pass on the advice Sally gave me. She said, "Go for it. Stick it out. Confront your fears. Accept your anger. Cry. Get support. Go through it. You have something needing doing. You have a task, a major task, to perform. It's as if you've been given this special assignment. Go through your grief with determination, as if you were swimming through a pool full of ice water. When you get to the other side, you'll feel incredibly different. You'll feel healed."

Thank you, Sally.

GRIEF AS HEALER—SOME SUGGESTIONS

Grief can heal the wounds we feel from the losses of life, especially the loss of a loved one. During those times of personal crisis, loving support is always helpful. I was fortunate to receive the following help-thoughts. As they helped me over the rough spots in my grief, so may they also help you.

Live each day to the maximum, one day at a time.

Allow yourself to rest and recuperate without becoming slobby.

Do something physical. Keep active.

Be daring. Do those things you have always wanted to do.

Don't be surprised if you do something "crazy."

Wear something that signals your mourning.

The work of grieving is in reviewing the memories and feelings and things associated with the departed soul. This is difficult, and it needs to be done.

Cry, cry and cry some more.

Get rid of his/her stuff. Pare your shared possessions down to the bone.

Rebuild your possessions on what supports your life, rather than on what locks you into memories.

Allow yourself the freedom to move to a new space, your space.

Keep a personal journal of your feelings and of whatever else you are going through in your grief. The journal becomes a way to externalize your feelings and becomes a mirror of your progress.

Find and use a support group that truly supports your life changes.

Take your time in getting into a new relationship. Savor each new person for who she/he is. Avoid comparisons to your loved one. Move from a position of strength, not weakness.

Use the joy, power and love you gain from utilizing your grief as a means for healing, as the foundation on which to build your new life.

Fill that emptiness you feel with love—love for life, love for God, love for self, love for others.

Enjoy your self because if you don't, who can?

Remember that what you are feeling as grief is all yours. It is within you. It wants to leave. Let it.

AFFIRMATIONS—STATEMENTS OF UNDERSTANDING

Some of the help-thoughts I received evolved through use into statements that reflected where I was in my thinking/feeling. By continually using these statements which affirmed my feelings and thoughts, I gained a clarity as to where my inner center was. By keeping aware of my center, my inner core of beliefs, I found it easier to get through those times when everything was confusing, overwhelming and intensely emotional. (Intense emotional experiences leave me feeling at a loss. Consequently, I appreciated having these affirmations around to help me get my bearings again.)

I believe that I am being utilized by the Lord to facilitate my loved one's soul's transition.

The grief I feel is mine. It is within me, comes from within me. The grief I feel is not caused by anyone else. It is mine. I feel it. I feed it. I release it.

It is okay to cry.

Grief is a process of elimination. What is not eliminated now will seek a way out later in a much stronger form. It's better to release it now.

It is my responsibility to my self and my duty to God/Infinite Love to use my discrimination when refilling the emptiness I feel from grieving. I choose the most positive and beneficial input.

I choose to use the shitty way I feel as compost for a richer, fuller life.

It's okay to feel good about grief, even though grief may not feel good.

Grief is the process, not the substance.

A challenge is both an obstacle and an opportunity.

I allow myself to heal. I do not need to define myself as broken or incomplete.

I am not my feelings. I am not my body. I am not my mind. I am a manifested soul who has a body, mind and feelings for creating good.

The more beauty I see in a loved one's death, the more beauty I see in my life.

I celebrate the release of a soul from this plane of existence; I celebrate the release of my attachments to the one who has left.

I trust in the Lord, and the Lord provides exactly what I need, whether I like it or not.

When someone dies there is no loss.
Their love abides in our heart all the time.

GERALD G. JAMPOLSKY, M.D.

THE KING IS DEAD!—LONG LIVE THE KING!

I've always enjoyed the irony of this expression, "The King is dead, long live the King." How can the King be dead and still be alive? In truth, the King never dies; it's the humans who play the part who come and go.

And so it has been in my life too. The woman who reflected my love has died. Yet love is still alive, awaiting a new player on the stage of my heart. The love we shared is still around. It did not die when Nancy died. Love is still with-in me and with-out me. Love is an energy, a formless energy, that permeates everything. Nancy's passing merely stopped our specific expression of love; but love itself did not die.

I miss our specific expression of love. How we hugged, how we kissed, how we played, how we disagreed, how we made love, how we opened the treasure troves of our individual lives to each other—that's what I miss. But that was all going to disappear anyway, it's just that I didn't expect it to happen so soon.

Most couples figure on being together into their sixties or more. Then it is expected that one or both will die. Death is part of growing old. When Nancy died, I was 42, definitely not old. Out of sheer youthful stubbornness, I decided to accept the whole situation as a challenge and an opportunity to learn all that I could about death and dying. By viewing her death as a basically positive event, I was able to transcend the quagmire that our emotions can become when involved in grief. This is not to say that I was not emotional. I still am. However, by accepting her death as a positive experience (for both of us) I was able to support her through her transition and was able to have my necessary emotional release without getting trapped in/by the process.

I didn't do it all on my own, though. I had a lot of help. Most of it came from teachers (people who had written books, people who had given seminars, people going through their grief and being stuck in it, and people going through their grief and not being stuck in it). The rest of it came from a willingness to go through it. There were times when I wanted a different kind of help than what I received. Specifically, there were times when I needed a fellow widower to talk with. What we would end up doing would be crying together just out of joy for having found a brother we felt safe enough to cry with. It's good we were able to do this, even though I also wanted to talk. So, instead of talking it out, I wrote it out. I suppose if I had talked more, I would have written less. So, it all balances out.

In my readings, I came across a story of another man whose wife had died. I find it uplifting. In fact, it, along with another similar story, kept me going when I felt I was completely alone in what I was going through. Here is the story, as related by Ron Boyer. The great Taoist master Chaung-Tze's beloved wife died. He accepted her death with remarkable equanimity. As guests arrived for the funeral rites, they found Chaung-Tze sitting on the front lawn, singing joyfully and drumming on an overturned bowl—hardly the solemn ceremony they had expected. An offended guest scolded him for his behavior; Chaung-Tze replied simply that "to break in upon her rest with the noise of lamentation would be to show I knew nothing of nature's sovereign law. At first, I felt saddened by her death. Then I realized that when born, she appeared out of nothing, and now she has simply returned to the same nothing."

I like this story because I play the drums and because it further supports the path I have followed in going through my grief process. It says that we have a choice as to how we can accept a loved one's death. We can accept it sour-fully, as did the offended guest who could not see past his own attachments, or we can accept it joyfully as did Chaung-Tze. He did not deny his sorrow; he too was saddened at first. But he moved past his sorrow and into his joy as he remembered nature's sovereign law—that which is, is either as form or as energy. He realized that his wife's soul essence "appeared out of nothing" to give her physical body life and consciousness and then "simply returned to the same nothing."

Even though it is always intense for us when we lose a friend or a loved one because in a sense, we are losing part of ourselves, the part which they reflected for us, we still are free, like Chaung-Tze, to express our joy over the release of their souls—without shame, without embarrassment and without feeling as if we are desecrating the dead. We too can move past our sorrow (and attachments) and into our joy at our realization of what has taken place—the transition of our loved one's soul from her/his physical body to the "nothing" (no-thing) of the spiritual realms. In New Orleans, when someone dies, the marching band accompanying their body to the cemetery plays slow, mournful dirges. But after the body is in the ground, the music soars, and the people dance.

In the book *A Course In Miracles,* we are challenged to relearn how to think. It gives step-by-step instruction in how to change our perceptions of what is going on both inside and outside of ourselves. Its arrival in human consciousness at this point in our evolution as a species is no accident. The lessons it offers have already changed many lives for the better. One of the things it teaches us is that to give is to receive. You reap not only what you sow, but also how you sow. Try applying this lesson when you find yourself dealing with grief. You can start by allowing yourself to express your grief with honesty, kindness and sensitivity, so that you cause no harm to either yourself or others. Allow yourself to view the beauty along with the ugliness. Allow yourself to see the opportunities for learning and growing offered you by your own unique grief process. Allow yourself to expand beyond your current views of death and life. And expect surprises!

Nancy's death opened my heart and challenged my mind.

I'm a different person now because of it. She taught me how to die right-eously by example, through her application of her years of spiritual and intellectual training to her own transition. She taught me how to live by giving me the situation in which I could recognize, sort out and deal with my fears and feelings.

Everything that happened between Nancy and me was perfect. Instead of fighting it, we learned to go with the flow of events. We brought our separate backgrounds to the process, added the teachings of Elisabeth Kubler-Ross, Stephen Levine, Ram Dass, Emanuel Swedenborg and others, and came up with an experience I can only liken to a very wild white-water raft trip in which the raft somehow manages to not tip over.

By going with the flow of events, I learned major soul lessons for myself: how to trust, how to love unconditionally, how to forgive, how to utilize my fears and how to give generously. Even though I feel I have more to complete within my grief process, it doesn't bother me anymore. I feel a newly uncovered confidence helping me rebuild my life while giving me strength to deal with the remaining layers.

It seems the Lord utilized me for two purposes: one was to aid and support Nancy as her soul made its transition from the physical plane (without hindering her by dwelling in our attachments), and the other was for learning what I needed in order to live the rest of my life in clarity and peace. Thank you, Lord. Thank you, Nancy. Thank you, all.

APPENDICES

APPENDIX I

The Ten Freedoms—Peter Schmidt (1931–1980)

You need not kill
You need not steal
You need not be unfaithful
You need not lie
You may love your father and mother
You need not desire other people's things
You need not desire other people's bodies
You need not make images
You may love God

APPENDIX II

The Tibetan Bardo System
(From *Who Dies?* by Stephen Levine)

There are many translations for the Tibetan word bardo, but essentially it means a passageway, a point of transition. Some define it as a gap, a space; others, as a portal. It is, it seems, another evolutionary stage, like the metamorphosis between phyla, a stage of transition from one moment to the next. Generally, we think of the bardos as occurring after death, but actually this moment is a bardo. We tend to think that such portals will become evident only after we drop the body, but that is only part of it. You are in a bardo at this very moment.

There are six bardos. The first of which is the Bardo of Birth; it is a moment of birth, an emergence bardo, if you will, the transitional experience of consciousness within a body moving into its own independent existence in this realm. The second bardo is the Lifetime Bardo; a bardo of becoming; the growth from child to adult; a bardo of learning and aging and the changes of a lifetime. This interval may be much shorter than the first or a hundred years longer. The bardo of life may also be thought of as the "empty-handed bardo"—a following of accumulated desires and goals, becoming what one wishes to be. The third bardo is of dissolution. It is the Bardo of the Moments Before Death. It is the transition out of the seemingly solid, a spacious withdrawal, a melting out of physical form into subtler realities.

The fourth is again a bardo of emergence. It is the Bardo of the Moments After Death. You will notice that there is no such thing as death but only the moments before and the moments after. The concept "death" has no basis in reality. For the body there is a moment when it is animated and a moment later when it has become a nonreturnable empty.

In *The Tibetan Book of the Dead*, it is in this fourth bardo, the transition after death—the emergence—that we often hear of the appearance of the great light called the Dharmata, where the essence of being, no longer identified with the confines of the body, shines before us. It is considered by many one of the most important and opportune times of an incarnation.

The fifth bardo, the Deathtime Bardo, is another of the roaming bardos, where we are in the transition to the next learning, aging, and growth that occurs as our mind runs off its conditioned content from a lifetime of holding and maneuvering for safety and security. It is an unraveling of the past, another opportunity to relate directly to the forms that arise in the mind and create our ways of seeing. It is in this bardo that many of the peaceful and wrathful deities are encountered. It is here that it is said that one meets the ten thousand loving and the ten thousand wrathful aspects of the mind. But, of course, these qualities are observable in our present bardo as well.

The sixth bardo, the Bardo of the Moment Before Birth, is again of dissolution. It is a moment of selecting a new birth, the choosing of incarnation. It is the moment when you are attracted to your next stage of becoming, when desires lead you to a new womb out of which to emerge into a world that most often seems too big or too small.

The use of the concepts of the bardo is a skillful means of pointing out that the illusion is happening right now wherever we are holding. It is also interesting to note that these bardos follow a certain process of arising (emergence), existence (a roaming) and dissolution; precisely the same as each state of mind that we notice arising, existing for a moment and passing away to give rise to the next emergence, existence and dissolution. Watching the moment-to-moment birth and death of the mind prepares us for whatever the next incarnation may be. It is watching this process of creation and dissolution that frees us from our sense of solidity, of "someone" to protect.

It is clear that the bardos of emergence are interchangeable. That birth and the moments after death are the same. That the bardos of existence roaming, of "life" and "death," are comprised of the same elements of consciousness and old tendencies. That the bardos of dissolution, of the moment before death and before birth are also interchangeable. Relating to each transition as it arises, we die from moment to moment into the Deathless.

APPENDIX III

The Needs of the Dying Person
(From *A Hospice Handbook* by Christine Longaker)

Below are listed some of the needs that a dying person may have. No one person will experience all of them.

1. To talk about their fears: of abandonment, intense pain, concern for family, or physical deterioration and dependence, and to allay these fears as much as possible.

2. To feel that dying is a natural process and that it is OK to let go. It is also normal to refuse food or further treatment when cure is no longer possible. If they desire, they can arrange with their doctor to avoid life-prolonging measures, while they are still conscious.

3. To know the diagnosis and prognosis, and to choose the type of care they want, with full knowledge of the consequences. They also have a right not to know, or deny full awareness of their condition.

4. To deal with increasing physical deterioration and dependence. Insisting on too much independence can add to stress and suffering. Permit them to maintain whatever dignity and control of self-care they can manage. Remember the need is for recognition as a human being, and not just as a body or disease.

5. To be treated as a whole person. This includes honoring many aspects of their life: emotional, spiritual, financial, self-image, physical, sexual, cultural, personal lifestyle, and rela-

tionships. Difficulties in one of these areas may cause more suffering to the person than their disease and its treatment.

6. To have their moods understood and accepted. To have others listen, without judging or explaining, to even the most difficult feelings: anger, despair, guilt, denial, resistance, or sorrow. Often prolonged anger and depression are covering up a deep feeling of sorrow and held-in grief at losing everything that is important to them.

7. To be at home as much as possible, or to feel at home. This can include little pleasures such as haircuts, plants, home-cooked meals, posters or music they enjoy, personal pajamas, and frequent visits by their close family and children, and intimate, private times with their partners.

8. To feel that their family can get along without them after their death. They need to be able to honestly communicate with family members what their feelings and needs are. They may want to cry with them while saying good-bye, and to have a few supportive people with whom they feel comfortable in silence or as they are dying. Completing unfinished business with someone, whether by talking or writing to them, will ease their minds and hearts.

9. To be as pain-free and alert as possible. Remember that psychological, emotional, or spiritual pain can accentuate the experience of physical pain. Because sleep patterns may change, some people may need to be awake at night.

10. To find a meaning for their lives, their suffering and their deaths. Sometimes a minister or priest can lend valuable assistance. Others need to discover this meaning on their own terms, and may need help in finding ways to give the days remaining to them a sense of purpose. Learning to experience their remaining days with full awareness and appreciation for life, coming to accept others and forgive those who have hurt them, letting go of attachments, offering their pain to God, or learning to communicate honestly with those they love—all these are things that a seriously ill or bedridden patient can still do to continue growing and participating in life.

11. To feel the respect and love of those who care for them.

This is shown by spending time with the dying person, and by allowing them to be themselves and to die in the way they choose. You can show caring by touching them, holding hands or giving backrubs, and by sharing your life, and sometimes your tears, with them. Though they may never say it, even the cranky or depressed person is appreciative of your continued visits when they feel your acceptance and love. By doing nothing more than listening, you may be doing more for them than you ever know.

12. To be treated as a living person, not a dying person. One way to validate the living is to recognize the needs for privacy, time alone with her or his family.

APPENDIX IV

The Needs of the Survivors
(From *A Hospice Handbook* by Christine Longaker)

1. They need to talk about their loved one and express their feelings to someone. There is nothing you need to say or do, just being there and listening is often enough.

2. To have their feelings accepted by someone who won't judge them or try to "explain away" their guilt or anger. These feelings may include: loneliness, fear, anger, sadness, apathy, numbness, guilt, despair, playfulness, feeling crazy, or overwhelmed. Sometimes they will feel like they are going crazy because they are not "in control" and do not understand their feelings—this is actually normal for such an intense loss. To be reassured that it is okay to mourn, and for a considerable time. Grief may be expressed through a need to get angry, to cry, or to escape for a while. The intensity of their pain will diminish, but not for a long time.

3. Healing takes time—it will not be over in a few weeks or months. The intense pain of their loss will reappear a few months after the death, at holidays, birthdays, and at the anniversary of the death. At the beginning, the experience of mourning is actually much like a serious illness that must be convalesced, slowly. Feelings like loneliness or guilt may surface long after the survivor feels they have recovered.

4. Someone who will continue to be there for them—calling or coming by, even after being told they are not needed initially.

This continuity is important at first, for it establishes a thread of caring they can depend on for a while. In time, trust builds, and they can ask for help when times get rough. The survivor will appreciate a person who shares themselves, their feelings and life, and who will go out with them occasionally.

5. At first, allow the survivor to withdraw from the world. At this time, they may need the most help with daily living activities: cooking, shopping, or childcare—to allow them to grieve. After some time has passed, they will want to take on more responsibilities, and gain full control over their lives again. Later, the need to withdraw will come up once in a while, and they should be encouraged to allow this much-needed "retreat."

6. To understand various types of reactions are normal while grieving:

Shortness of breath	Muscle aches
Poor concentration	Dry mouth
Irrational thoughts	Preoccupation with images
Feeling disoriented	of the deceased
Skin temperature	Dizziness
changes	Sighing
Nausea	Tiredness
Loss of appetite	Racing heartbeat

7. To recognize and get past the barriers to expressing their grief:

A fear of going crazy if they let it all out.

Judging that they are just "feeling sorry for themselves."

Guilt that they wished the person to die, or did not love them enough.

Feeling that they should be over it by now (whether it has been weeks, months, or years since the death).

Deciding they should be strong, and in control of themselves.

Feeling distressed by the demands of too many well-meaning people around or feeling isolated when they all leave.

Afraid to let children see their grief.

Worried about a job, financial security, or angry at the deceased because they are left with all the responsibilities.

8. Certain kinds of deaths bring out more intense reactions in grief: sudden deaths, suicide, or the death of a child. There will be greater shock, much more guilt, strong anger, and feelings of despair or helplessness. Survivors will fear they are really going crazy when these strong emotions seem to overwhelm them. They will need reassurance that someone will be there to make sure they won't go too far, and that it is best to talk out the thoughts which are most upsetting. Sleep patterns may change, causing alarm also.

9. The expression of grief includes many feelings that seem abnormal. Only when certain feelings really interfere with a person's life for an unusually long period of time, is there a problem that may require professional help. Some of these are: prolonged feelings of guilt, mourning that is repressed, extreme fear of the world, extreme identification with the deceased person's illness, continued denial of the death, or not being able to care for one's self or one's children. With high-grief deaths, even these reactions are normal and for a time careful consideration should be given before suggesting additional help.

10. After the initial mourning has begun, the survivor can begin to set one or two short-term goals. They can learn new skills, resume old projects, or get involved in a few social activities. It is also important to get exercise and stay healthy during this time. Some of the resources for support are: past interests or jobs, career guidance, community groups, volunteer work, colleges, skill training, re-entry programs, ministers, close family members, professional advisors, support groups for survivors (Family Services, Hospice), treating themselves to something new.

11. Learning to assert themselves. To re-enter the world, they must learn to communicate their needs and feelings, to

ask for favors sometimes, and develop skills that will help them to live effectively in the world. Developing these qualities will balance the temporary feelings of helplessness and immobility that surface from time to time.

ACKNOWLEDGMENTS

Acknowledgment is made to the following for their kind permission to reprint copyrighted material:

Shirley MacLaine, *Out on a Limb,* copyright 1983 by Shirley MacLaine. Reprinted by permission of Bantam Books, Inc., New York, NY.

Elisabeth Kubler-Ross, *On Death and Dying,* copyright 1970 by Elisabeth Kubler-Ross. Reprinted by permission of Macmillan Publishing Co., New York, NY.

Samuel Warren, *A Compendium of Swedenborg's Theological Writings,* copyright 1979 by the Swedenborg Foundation, Inc. Reprinted by permission of the Swedenborg Foundation, Inc., New York, NY.

Emanuel Swedenborg, *Heaven and Hell,* translated by George Dole, copyright 1971, 1979, Dole translation, by the Swedenborg Foundation, Inc. 1984 edition. Reprinted by permission of the Swedenborg Foundation, Inc., New York, NY.

Sogyal Rinpoche, "Gates of Death," copyright 1981 by the Laughing Man Institute. Reprinted courtesy of *The Laughing Man* magazine, 750 Adrian Way, San Rafael, CA, 94903. All rights reserved.

The Scriptural quotations contained herein are from the *Revised Standard Version of the Bible,* copyright 1946, 1952, 1971 by the Division of Christian Education of the National Council of the Churches of Christ in the U.S.A. and are used by permission. All rights reserved.

Mikhail Naimy, *The Book of Mirdad, The Strange Story of a Monastery Which Was Once Called the Ark,* copyright 1962 by Mikhail Naimy. 1984 edition. Reprinted by permission of Clear Press, London, in association with Element Books, Salisbury.

Christine Longaker, *A Hospice Handbook: Caring for the Dying and Their Families* by Christine Longaker, copyright 1980. Thesis from University of California at Santa Cruz. Excerpts reprinted by permission of Christine Longaker, Santa Cruz, CA.

Acknowledgment is made to the following for their kind permission to reprint various material:

Ram Dass for his story about the monk.

Barney Munger for his photograph of Nancy Pema Madson Elmer on which the drawing is based.

The estate of Tim Monaghan for his remarks and observations.

Rev. Randall Laakko for his quotes which helped so much.

Danaan Perry for his quote given during one of his wonderful talks.

Gerald G. Jampolsky, M.D., for his quote given during his seminar.

The estate of Peter Schmidt for "The Ten Freedoms," and the basic head drawing found in his book, *Im Kopf—In the Head*.

ABOUT THE AUTHOR

Lon Elmer lives in Seattle, where he is a writer and business consultant. He has been a longshoreman, advertising copy-writer, professional musician, director of drug rehabilitation programs, counsellor and teacher. He enjoys sailing, river rafting, circuses and old cars.